HF335072

Emotional intelligence and personality as moderators of work-life balance and mental health of women managers

ACKNOWLEDGEMENTS

First and foremost I express my gratitude to Allah (SWT) for giving me strength and courage to complete the journey of my Ph.D. and always being a source of light and positivity to handle the challenges of the journey.

I would like to express my sincere gratitude to my guide and supervisor, Dr. Meena Osmany. I thank her for being so patient with the ups and downs of my Ph.D. journey and always encouraging me to do good work and learn new things. Without your guidance and support, it would not have been possible for me to complete the Ph.D. Thesis. As a teacher, you extracted best out of me and helped me grow as a researcher and as a person. Thank you Ma'am!

I would also like to thank my Head of the Department, Prof. M. G. Shahnawaz, for his continuous encouragement and support. I thank you Sir for organizing all the statistical workshops in the department and always encouraging us to do good work in our Ph.D. research. In addition, I also thank entire faculty members and office staffs for their contribution in my Ph.D. Journey.

I extend my special thanks to Aseem Kumar Sir, Shrikant P. Bhande Sir, Rahman Sir, Mr. Matloob Hasan, Mr. Mahatabuzzaman, Archana Ma'am and Nupur Jain Ma'am for their immense support in the data collection of my Ph.D. work. My sincere thanks go to all the participants of the study who spared their precious time in completing the questionnaires and interviews.

I am especially and deeply grateful to my dearest parents for their unconditional love and support throughout my education. It is difficult to express my gratitude in words for my "Papa" Late Md. Gholam Shahid who always believed in me and allowed me to fly with my wings of dreams and ambitions. You are the source of inspiration and the role model of my life. You will always be alive in my heart!

I want to extent my special thanks to my beloved husband Md. Fazle Ali for being a constant source of support throughout my Ph.D. journey. This Ph.D. is the result of your tireless effort, patience and limitless love. I also want to thank my "Bundle of joy" my five year old son Mohammad Aaquib, who needed me most when I was busy with my books and laptop. You are best son in this world, who made your Mom a stronger woman. I am also greatly thankful to my In-laws "Ammi & Abba" for their blessings and support, which helped me in pursuing my Ph.D. with my early years of motherhood.

My family is incomplete without mentioning the name of my loving siblings, Gholam Tajdar, Meraj Anwer, Saima Taj and Ayesha Taj. I want to say you "thank you" for believing in me and always being there for me, when I needed you. I love you all.

Last but not the least, I would like to extend my thanks to my valuable friends Sabeen Fatima Rizwi, Nazia Talat, Shaheena Aapi, Shahid Bhai, Mohammad Imran, Nasrina Siddiqui, Imtiyaz, and Anjuman Bains for their valuable inputs in my Ph.D. research work and making the entire journey a memorable and nostalgic experience for me.

I am deeply sorry for not being able to mention each and every person who helped me to make this journey complete. I sincerely thank them all for their support and help.

LIST OF TABLES

LIST OF FIGURES

1.1 Work-life balance: key issues

Work-life balance can be defined as the effective management of multiple responsibilities at work, at home, and in the other aspects of life (Naithani, 2010). Though the concept of work-life balance is quite old in origin, which can be traced back to pre-industrialization period, over the past two decades, the issues of work-life balance have received extensive publicity in the industry as well as in the area of research (Eby et.al. , 2005; Hogarth et.al.,2000). Concerns about work –life balance have become important for the employees as well as for the organizations due to number of reasons. In modern work environment, the prevailing cut-throat competition and emerging trend of "996" work culture have made work-life balance a major issue for every working professional. Today majority of the working populations are living with nuclear families where social support is inadequate and life is dependent on technology. This technology has made their life easier in many ways, but it has also created expectations for constant availability at work and in the family at same time. Computers, Smart phones, Skype, What's App and other advances in information technology have made possible to create virtual work-environment anywhere, which has allowed work demands to intrude into family and personal life. Furthermore, global competition has increased pressure on organizations and individual employees to be more flexible and adaptive towards change (Hall & Moss 1998). In strive to become more competitive, companies often go for de-layering, outsourcing, downsizing and understaffing (Dunford,1999 & Sparrow, 2000), due to which employees of these companies and their families face fear of job loss, low wages, increased work load and diminishing sense of control over work (Grosswald el al.,2001 & Sparks et al.,2001). In this climate, high work stress and stress related illness are common in employees, which makes achieving work-life balance even more challenging (Jones & Bright, 2001).

1.2. Work-life balance and its importance

The issue of work-life balance is important for employees as well as for the organizations. The conflict between work and personal life results in many negative health outcomes including stress, depression and anxiety disorders, which adversely affect their performance at workplace (Yucel, 2017; Wang Li, 2006). Hence, maintaining a good balance between work and personal life is important to ensure individual and organizational success.

Previously, it was assumed that the concept of work-life balance is applicable to women only, but in recent studies it has been found that the construct is applicable to professionals of both genders at various levels of their professional careers (Armour, 2005; Blair-Loy, 2003). Both men and women prefer working in those organizations which support their work-life balance (Burke, 2002). The reason is obvious, work-life balance is not only essential for good mental health and well-being of the employees, it also results in various positive outcomes in workplace.

According to Naithani (2010), employees having better work-life balance, contribute more meaningfully towards the organizational goal and success. Ahmed (2014) in his study on 200 employees working in telecommunication industry in Pakistan found that, work-life balance support job satisfaction which leads to lower turnover intension in the employees.

Similarly, Scholarios and Marks (2004) in their study on software professionals found that even these professional are unlikely to show strong attachment with single organization for a longer period of time, family friendly policies make them more committed to the organizations and also enhance their job satisfaction. It results in low employee turnover in the organization which eventually saves the high cost incurred in the training and development of these hi-tech professionals.

Work-life balance leads to productive and innovative employees in the organization (Greenhaus, 2003), while disparity in the work-life balance tends to develop distressed and dissatisfied employees (Kofodimos, 1993). When work-life imbalance and mental health issues develop in employees they tend to develop further issues such as depression, negative emotions, low energy, pessimism, fatigue and sleep disorders (Hamming & Bauer, 2009).

The impact of work-family conflict and other manifestations of work stress is not only restricted to the individual employees but evidences show that it also affect partners and other family members- a phenomenon is called "crossover". Hammer, Allen and Grigsby (1997) examined crossover in a sample of bank employees and found that there is a bidirectional crossover of work-family conflict from husbands to wives and vice versa. Westman, Vinokur, Hamilton and Roziner (2004) examined crossover in Russian officers and their wives and found a strong crossover of marital dissatisfaction from husband to wives but no crossover from wives to husbands, demonstrating the traditional gender role ideology in dual-career family. Studies related to crossover are mainly focused on five major strains: physical health, burnout, depression, work-family conflict, anxiety and dissatisfaction. However some researchers have detected instances of positive crossover between the partners as well. For example, Bakker, Demerouti and Schaufeli (2005) in their study on 323 couples found a positive crossover of work engagement (vigor and dedication) between the partners, which expanded the previous research on crossover by showing positive experiences at work transferred to home domain.

1.3. Recent changes in work-force demographics in India

In last twenty five years, India has experienced rapid economic growth, increased educational attainment, and urbanization (Lahoti & Swaminathan, 2013). Increased educational enrollment and social changes have resulted in more women entering into the workforce, but surprisingly, the participation of Indian women in the workforce fell 10% in the past decade. The number of working women increased during 2000-2005, reaching 34% to 37%, but the rate has reduced continuously thereafter and reached 27% in 2014 (IANS, 2016).

The persistent decline in female labour force participation rate (LFPR) in India in the face of consistent economic growth is a puzzling phenomenon. Between the second employment-unemployment survey conducted in 2011-12 and the latest round in 2015-16, participation of women in the labour force has declined and unemployment has risen. Only 23.7% of eligible Indian women are part of the workforce, compare that to 75% of men. In urban areas, this number drops further to only 16%. For men, the comparable number is 69%. Even for those women who are part of the workforce, the unemployment rate is high. 8.7% compared to 4 percent for men (NSSO,2016). The Global Gender Gap Report 2018 by the World Economic Forum ranked India at 142 out of 149 countries. Syria, Pakistan, Iraq and Yemen are among the few that rank below India.

The decline in women's economic activity is a matter of concern to those who are concerned for women's well being as well as those who believe that women are valuable resources and must be utilized efficiently. Women's employment is a critical factor in their progression towards economic independence and is also considered as an indicator of their overall status in society (Mammen and Paxson 2000).

In India, Women's participation in the labour market is influenced by social norms governing gender roles and responsibilities as much as it is by economic and structural factors (Lahoti & Swaminathan, 2013).There are certain primary reasons for low participation of women in the labour force like lack of access to higher education among women, dearth of opportunities to work and inflexible working conditions. Lack of flexibility in working conditions tends to dissuade women from joining the labour force as they turn to their domestic duties (Assocham,2016). The cultural traditions and family role structures have not changed significantly and women on average still bear responsibilities for daily household chores, such as cooking, shopping, providing care for children and aged family members (Kalliath, 2011).

1.4 Women at managerial position

Since the 1970s, the role of women went through a sea change in Indian society. Women started becoming more aware of their personal needs and demanding their equal status both within the home and outside. They started joining the labour force for paid works and also made their place in Indian business world as managers and entrepreneurs. Today women comprise 23.7% of labour workforce (NSSO, 2016) in India, but despite of educational attainment and professional skills, women are still less likely to hold managerial position than men. Recently, the Confederation of Indian Industry released a report indicating that women comprise only 16% of junior managers, 4% of middle and senior managers and a mere 1% of organizational leaders. Thus, while women are adequately represented in the workforce at large, they remain barely present in managerial positions (CSR, 2017).

The underrepresentation of women in management is not unique to India, it is a global issue for many developed countries like USA, Canada, New Zealand, Australia and Israel, but the scenario is much better than India. The term "Glass ceiling" was coined in United States during 1970s to describe the invisible artificial barriers, created by attitudinal and organizational prejudices, which block women to reach up to senior executive positions. In year 2002, 38% American women were more likely to work in managerial occupation than men (28%), while men (42%) were still more likely than women (33%) to supervise other employees as a major part of their jobs (Bond et al. 2002). In Canada 10.8% of employed women held a management position, and only 19.1% of senior-level managers were women (HRD Canada, 2001). In New Zealand, only 11% of women in paid employment work as legislators, administrators and managers compared to 15% of the men. Australian statistics reveal that only 3.6% of employed women held managerial and administrative position compared to 9.5 % of employed men (Commonwealth Office of the Status of Women, 2001). In Israel, only 22% of country's managers are women and of that only 8% are on top management while in contrast 33% of male managers are on top level management (Israel Central Bureau of Statistics, 2000).

Whether this glass ceiling occurs in the workplace or in politics it is actually a reflection of social and economic gender inequality. A major source of discrimination stems from strongly held attitudes towards women's and men's social roles and behavior (ILO, 2001). According to Loughlin (1999), there are vast amount of available literature on barriers to women's career progression, but work-life balance is one of the key factors that affects women's and men's career differently.

For women the major obstacle which hinders them to be on the top position is the critical balancing act of combining a family and a career (Cross, 2010; Gupta et al., 1998). Although men also face this challenge of balancing work and other priorities, it affects women more since they do most of the work associated with the household activities, apart from taking care of children, older family members, and other dependents (Rehman & Roomi, 2012 ; Poelmans, 2001).They deal with "Double life perspective" between career and children where they have to make choices between career and children (Bakkar, 2000). Women's life cycle pattern for childbearing and career progression in senior management ladder is diametrically opposite. The demanding career stage years, when they are expected to show high work commitments to succeed, often coincide with their biological child bearing years

(Drew, 2005). These multiple demands in work and family eventually lead to role conflict, overload, and stress (Ram, Khoso, Shah, Chandio & Shaikih, 2011; Pevney, 2004). In the long run, the success for these women is often at substantial cost to their personal lives. Due to demanding job, they have to work very long hours and may have to forgo long-term relationships and the opportunity to have children if they wish to progress to the top of the profession (Mahal, 2014).

1.5 Motivation for the study (Rationale)

Work-life balance is an important aspect of women's life which has a great influence on her family, career and health. Today women are working at all level in the hierarchy of organizations, but those who are working at managerial positions are under high pressure and job demands. At professional domain, they have the responsibility of leadership roles. They also face an invisible barrier "glass ceiling" that blocks them rising above certain level in organizations created by corporate tradition and prejudice (Crampton & Mishra, 2000). Although they are qualified as their male counterparts, sometimes they need to work harder and perform better to obtain senior positions (Still, 1994; and Maddock, 2002). A subtle form of discrimination is also reported, it has been found that male employees could not accept the idea to work under a female manager (Sheth, 1997). On other hand, at family domain they still continue to have the primary responsibilities of taking care of the children, dependent elders and household needs. Conflict arises when demands from work and family roles are mutually incompatible, such that participation in one role makes it difficult to participate in the other (Liu & Wilson, 2001). Women managers often deal with "Double life perspective" between career and children where they have to make choices between career and children (Bakkar, 2000). Women's life cycle pattern for childbearing and career progression in senior management ladder is diametrically opposite. The demanding career stage years, when they are expected to show high work commitments to succeed, often coincide with their biological child bearing years (Drew, 2005). These multiple demands in work and family eventually lead to role conflict, stress and depression which adversely affect their mental health (Yucel, 2017; Ram, Khoso, Shah, Chandio & Shaikih, 2011). Hence, it is critical to see the issues of work-life balance through the lenses of Psychology. There is a need to explore potential moderators which can buffer the negative impact of conflict on the mental health of women managers. From the perspective of "Conservation of resource (COR) theory" emotional intelligence and personality characteristics can be assumed as personal resources which have the potential to weaken the negative impact of conflict on mental health. Hence, the present study examines the moderating role of emotional intelligence and personality on the relationship of work-life balance and mental health of women managers. Apart from this, the present study also attempts to fill important gaps in work-life balance literature. First, earlier studies on work-life balance were mainly focused on work-family conflict and family work-conflict. Later, from the view of positive psychology, it was argued that work and family are not always a source of conflict, but they can be also the source of growth and support for each other. Hence, there is also need to study the facilitation/enhancement part of work-life balance. In the present study work-life balance will be studied as a broader theme, which will include three dimensions of work-life balance; work interference with personal life, personal life interference with work and work/personal life enhancement. Second, though the issues related to work life balance have been widely researched in United Kingdom, USA, Australia, New Zealand and other countries of the world, yet in India, not much research has been done and it is not easy to find references to work life balance policies and practices in context of women managers. In fact, many women who are experiencing work-family conflict in their own lives fail to recognize this as a problem that can be resolved (Desai, 2003). The present study will explore work-family and mental health issues of women managers in Indian context both quantitatively as well as qualitatively. The quantitative study will be conducted to see the correlation between the study variables and analyzing probable moderators like emotional intelligence and personality from the perspective of "Conservation of Resource (COR)" theory, while qualitative study will be conducted to assess underlying perceptions, beliefs and personal experiences of women managers regarding their work-life balance and mental health issues. Hence, the present study will address work-life balance and mental health issues of Indian women managers from a broader perspective and help them to achieve better work-life balance and mental health. In addition, it will also test the conservation of resource theory in context of work-life balance in Indian work-family culture to ensure its generalizability beyond the western culture.

2.1. Work-life balance: evolution of the concept

The concept of work-life balance has evolved through different phases of work and family life spheres at different period of time. In early years of communal living (Phase 1) entire family used to be engaged in work for its sustenance, work was a part of family life (Carlson et al. 2005). Gradually, during pre-industrialization period (Phase 2) partial segregation started between the work and family life due to growth of trade and craft businesses. After industrial revolution in mid 1800s (Phase 3) use of heavy machines and mass production necessitated establishing factories away from home which further strengthened the segregation between work and family life. Men dominated the workforce while women were mainly engaged in taking care of children and house hold activities (Voydanoff, 2006). During late 18th and early 19th century (Phase 4) due to division of labour and between early 19th century and 1950s (Phase 5) due to technological factors which mainly dependent on physical strength gave men priority over women at workplace. Hence men took the role of bread earner while women confined in family domain only (Snooks, 1996).

A critical turn took place during second half of the 20th century (Phase 6), when technological advancement and computerization reduced the dependency of physical strength in the factories and facilitated the entries of women at work place (Snooks,1996). Division of gender reversed and more and more women started joining the workforce. During 1980s and 1990s (Phase 7) companies started offering family friendly programs especially for supporting working mothers (Lockwood, 2003). Later in early years of 21st century, these programs became less gender specific as companies started recognizing other commitment of life as well (Lockwood, 2003).

During 1950s to early 21st century, it was realized that gender as a sole factor does not influence work and family issues but other socio-economic factors are also influencing the work and personal life of the employees. According to Nathani and Jha (2009) three important categories of such factors were: family and personal life related factors (child care, elder care, personal health etc.) work related factors (long working hours, organizational culture etc.) and other factors (technology, social support etc.). Hence, a broader discourse of "work-life balance" emerged in work-family sphere, where practitioners and researchers started recognizing a broader aspect of life. Byrne (2005) presented "work-life balance" as balanced wheel of life which include work, finances, spiritual, hobbies, self, social, family and health. Work-life balance was defined as achieving balance between these important sections of life (Byrne 2005). He treated all the eight sections of life with equal weight, which is not true for every individual. Addressing to this limitation, Naithani (2010) defined work-life balance as the effective management of multiple responsibilities at work, at home, and in the other aspects of life. He argued that work-life balance has long- term relevance for individual employees as well as the employing organization. Work-life balance results into highly engaged and productive employees which meaningfully contribute to qualitative and quantitative organizational performance (Naithani & Jha, 2009).

2.1.1. Work-life balance: Important theories

To explain the phenomenon of work-life discourse, different theories have been proposed through researchers and scholars in the literature. Early researchers treated work and family as separate domains. During 1970s, open-system theories (compensation theory, spillover theory) were developed which hypothesized that work and family life influence each other, so employees, employers and society cannot ignore one sphere without potential influence to the other (Swarnlatha, 2017). An overview of important theories of work-life balance is presented below:

A. Segmentation theory: This theory assumes that work and family are two segmented domains and do not affect each other. The separation in time, space and function allows the individuals to fairly separate their personal and professional life. The pioneers of this theory were Blood and Wolf (1960), who applied this perspective to blue collar workers. They argued that for workers involved in unsatisfying and unengaged jobs, segmentation of work and family domain is very natural. The family is seen as a domain of relationships, affection and intimacy, while work domain is seen as impersonal, competitive and instrumental. Later, this view was challenged by researchers who empirically demonstrated that work and family life of an individual is not segmented, rather they are interrelated and affected by each other (Bruke & Greenglass, 1987; Voydanoff, 1987).

B. Compensation theory: The compensation theory argued that there is a complementary relationship between work and family domain. Workers try to compensate the lack of satisfaction in one domain (work or family) by attaining more satisfaction in another domain (Lambert, 1990). For example, to overcome job dissatisfaction worker may choose to actively participate in his/her social life. Two types of compensation had been observed in literature. First, a person may decrease his/her involvement in less satisfying domain and increase involvement is relatively high satisfying domain (Lambert, 1990). Second, the person may compensate dissatisfaction in one domain by pursuing rewards in the other domain (Champoux, 1978). The latter form of compensation can be either supplemental or reactive in nature (Zedeck, 1992). In supplement compensation, individuals shift their desire of rewarding experience in less satisfying domain to potentially more satisfying domain. For example, employees having less autonomy at workplace seek more autonomy in their personal life. In reactive compensation, individuals try to compensate their negative experiences in one domain by pursuing contrasting experience in another domain. For example, after a bad day in office, a person seeks to involve in recreational activities at home.

C. Instrumental theory: The instrumental theory suggests that activities in one domain are means to facilitate reward in other domain (Guest, 2002). For example, a worker may opt for a monotonous job to maximize his earning to buy a home for his family.

D. Conflict theory: This theory is based on "role conflict" model proposed by Kahn et.al. (1964). Role conflict is defined as "simultaneous occurrence of two (or more) sets of pressures such that compliance with one would make more difficult compliance with the other" (Kahn et. al.1964). Based on role conflict theory, Greenhaus and Beutell (1985) defined work-family conflict as "a form of inter role conflict in which the role pressures from work and family domains are mutually incompatible in some respect, that is, the participation in the work(family) is made more difficult by virtue of participation the family (work) role". Conflict between work and family can be bi-directional: work-family conflict and family-work conflict (Frone et. al., 1992a; Greenhaus & Beutell, 1985). Work-family conflict (WFC) occurs when demands of work are incompatible with family needs. For example, long working hours, work overload may interfere with taking care of family responsibilities at home. Similarly, family-work conflict (FWC) occurs when family demands are incompatible with work demands. For example, presence of young kids and unsupportive family members may interfere with fulfilling work commitment on time.

E. Spillover theory: This theory hypothesized that work and family domain are interrelated. One domain influences the other in a positive or negative way (Guest 2002). Research shows that individuals carry the emotions, attitudes, skill and behaviors established at work into their family life and vice –versa (Belsky et. al, 1985; Crouter, 1984). Positive spillover occurs when positive experiences of one domain like achievement and happiness etc. are transferred into the another domain, while negative spillover occurs when negative experiences like fatigue, depression etc. are transferred into the another domain (Xu,2009).

F. Work/family Border theory: Clark (2000) introduced a new theory of work-life balance called work/family border theory. According to this theory, primary connection between work and family systems is not emotional but human. The different domains of life specially work and family are separated by borders, which can be physical, temporal and psychological in nature. Everyday people cross this border while making transactions between domain of work and domain outside work. People try to mold these borders and shape their environment and in turn shaped by them. Work/family border theory explains this complex interaction between people and their different domains of life, to predict the conditions of conflict, and provide a framework to achieve balance (Clark, 2000).

2.1.2. Work-life balance: Important models

A number of conceptual models of work-life balance have been proposed by eminent scholars in the field of work-family literature (Greenhaus & Beutell, 1985;Guest, 2002;

Voydanoff, 2005; Greenhaus & Powell, 2006), which explain the different perspectives of work-life balance discourse.

Greenhaus and Beutell (1985) proposed a model on work-family conflict, which explains the important sources of conflict. According to this model there are three major source of work-family conflict: a) time based conflict, b) strain based and c) behavior based conflict. Time based conflict occurs when time pressure associated with one role makes it difficult to participate effectively in other roles. Strain based conflict occurs when strain caused due to one role interfere with effective participation in another role. Behavioral based conflict occurs when behavior required performing one role is incompatible with behavior required performing another role. According to the model the sources of conflict at work domain are: number of working hours, role conflict, role ambiguity, inflexible work schedule and expectations for objectivity and confidentiality. While, sources of conflict at family domain are: number of children, spouse employment, lack of spouse support, family conflict, expectation for warmth and openness.

Guest (2002) proposed a model which explored the determinants of work-life balance in work, home and individual context. According to the model, determinants of work and home are; demands of work, culture of work, demands of home and culture of home. Individual determinants include age, gender, personality, life and career stage, work-orientation, energy, personal control and coping. The model also explained nature, causes and outcomes of work-life balance. It defined work-life balance both subjectively and objectively. The objective indicators included time (number of hours) spent at work and time spent at personal life. Subjective indicator referred to individual's state of balance and imbalance. It is an individual's choice to give preference to one domain (work or family) over the other or giving equal weight to both the domains. Work-life balance is defined as achieving balance between the two domains. The model also reported outcomes of work-life balance which included enhanced performance in work and home, personal satisfaction and well-being.

Voydanoff (2005) proposed a conceptual model based on person-environment fit theory that linked work, family, and boundary-spanning demands and resources to work and family role performance and quality. The linking mechanism included two dimensions of perceived work-family fit (work demands-family resources fit and family demands-work resources fit) and a global assessment of perceived work-family balance. It has been found that, work-family and boundary-spanning demands and resources are associated with the two dimensions of fit, which combine with boundary-spanning strategies to influence work-life balance, which in turn affects role performance and quality.

Greenhaus and Powell (2006) proposed a theoretical model of work-family enrichment. They defined work-family enrichment as the extent to which experiences in one role improves the quality of life in the other role. Work-family enrichment occurs through two paths: instrumental path and affective path. The model assumed that resources generated in one role (role A) promote high performance and positive affects in another role (role B) and vice-versa. Through instrumental path resources can transferred directly from role A to role B thus, enhancing performance in role B. This path is moderated by salience of Role B, perceived relevance of resources to Role B and Consistency of resources with requirements and norms of Role B. Through affective path, resources generated in Role A can promote positive affect within Role A which in turn enhances performance and positive affect in Role B. This path is moderated by salience of Role B only.

On the basis of above mentioned theories and models it can be concluded that work-life balance is a complex psychological construct, which is influenced by many factors like; work related factors, family related factors, personal factors and external factors (moderators and mediators). Hence, it needs to be examined thoroughly from psychological perspective to make it manageable for individuals and organizations and get benefited from its positive outcomes.

2.2. Mental health: Evolution of the concept

Earlier concept of "Mental health" was often associated with psychological problems, illness and complaints. After World War Second, discipline of psychology went through a sea change. The professionalization and scientific growth of field yielded many trends to study mental health (Lunt, 1999). Many psychologist started working as qualified practitioner after taking proper recognition and training. Growth of subfields like Clinical psychology and Health psychology developed many models to treat disorders and illnesses. For example, medical model of health psychology diagnosed mental health from perspective of psychopathology and maladaptive behaviors. This model has many advantages, as it studied and understood the risk factor which causes these disorders. It also helped in developing valid and reliable instruments to measure mental disorders and most importantly, it led to pharmacological and psychological intervention to treat psychological disorders and illnesses (Seligman & Csikszentmihalyi, 2000). While having many advantages, the model suffered from some shortcomings. For example, the approach is accompanied by the risk that the person under diagnosis may reduce to the sum of his or her problems. Further, the categorization of mental disorders led to misleading assumption that normal behavior can be distinguished from abnormal behavior and mental disorder can qualitatively be distinguished from normal functioning and from other disorders (Widiger & Samuel, 2005). Another disadvantage of classification of mental disorder is that it leads to stigmatization, due to which people hesitate to seek help and participate in health care programs. Hence, apart from viewing mental health from medical point of view, there is a need to explore it from other perspective as well.

In the present thesis we studied "mental health" from perspective of positive psychology. According to World Health Organization, mental health can be defined as "A state of well-being in which the individual realizes his or her own abilities, can cope with the normal stresses of life, can work productively and fruitfully, and is able to make a contribution to his or her community" (WHO, 2005). Hence, a holistic approach to understand mental health should not focus into treating illnesses only, but also promoting well-being by focusing on individual goals and strengths in the person (Slade, 2010).

The present trend of studying "positive mental health" is based on two ancient tradition of well-being: hedonism and eudemonia. The hedonic approach focuses on "happiness" and defines well-being as experiencing maximum amount of pleasure and avoidance of pain in life, while eudemonic approach focuses on one's own potential and defines well being as optimal functioning and self-realization (Ryan & Deci, 2001). These two traditions of research on well –being conceptualized three component of well-being: emotional well-being, psychological well-being and social well-being. All these three components of well-being constitute the definition of positive mental health (Lamers, 2012).

2.2.1 Mental health: Important models

On the basis of research, **Marie Jahoda (1958**) proposed a multidimensional model of mental health in which she described six dimensions of mental health: a) Attitudes of an individual towards his/her own self; b) the degree of growth, development and self-actualization; c) coherence and continuity of personality; d) autonomy and self-determination; e) adequate perception of reality and f) environmental mastery.

Carol Ryff (1989), on the basis of eudemonic tradition, proposed a model on psychological well-being to define mental health, which included six dimensions: a) self-acceptance; b) positive relations with others; c) personal growth; d) purpose in life; e) autonomy; and f) environmental mastery.

Keyes (1998) argued that mental health is not a private phenomenon, it gets influenced by social structure, social ties and, social task and challenges. Hence, he proposed concept of social well-being to define mental health. He conceptualized his multidimensional model of social well-being on five dimensions: a.) social contribution b.) social integration c.) social acceptance d.) social actualization and e.) social coherence.

Empirical evidence of factor analysis showed that, these dimensions did not overlap with measures of emotional well-being and psychological well-being, so social well-being emerged as one of the distinct components of well-being to define one's mental health.

Vaillant (2003), on the basis of theories of positive psychology, proposed six different criteria to conceptualize mental health: a) mental health as above normal; b) mental health as positive psychology; c) mental health as maturity; d) mental health as social-emotional intelligence; e) mental health as subjective well-being; and f) mental health as resilience.

On the basis of above mentioned models it can be concluded that "mental health" is a multidimensional complex phenomenon, which is influenced by person's inner self, perception towards self and outer environment and social factors.

2.2.2. Mental health and work-life balance

In the present thesis we are attempting to explore a direct relationship between work-life balance and mental health of women managers, however literature shows many studies which established direct or indirect relationship between work-life balance and dimensions of mental health like stress, anxiety, depression, well-being etc. in other populations.

For example, Haar, Russo, Sune and Ollier-Malaterre (2014) conducted their study on 1416 employees from seven different populations-Malaysian, Spanish, French, New Zealand European, New Zealand Maori, Chinese, and Italian. They investigated the effect of work-life balance (WLB) on individual outcomes like job satisfaction, life satisfaction and depression across the culture and found that, work-life balance was positively related to job and life satisfaction, while negatively related to anxiety and depression in all seven populations. Further the SEM analysis showed that Individualism/ collectivism and gender egalitarianism moderated the relationship between WLB and individual outcomes.

Positive relationship of WLB with job and life satisfaction was stronger for respondents of individualistic culture in compare to respondents of collectivistic culture. Positive relationship of WLB with job and life satisfaction; and negative relationship of WLB with anxiety were stronger for respondents in gender egalitarian culture. Overall the study found work-life balance beneficial for employees of all seven cultures.

Deniz Yucel (2017) applied stress-divorce model to test the impact of work-family balance on marital satisfaction (stress spillover) of 1,961 married participants of USA, and examined that whether this effect is mediated by mental and physical health of the participant. Results suggested that respondents who experienced high work-family conflict have lower marital satisfaction, whereas those who experienced high work-family enrichment have higher marital satisfaction. Further, it has been found that both mental and physical health fully mediate the effect of work-to-family conflict, while mental and physical health both partially mediate the effect of work-to-family enrichment on marital satisfaction. Neither of the health measure (mental & physical health) mediated the effect of family-to-work conflict and family-to-work enrichment on marital satisfaction. This study also signified the importance of work-life balance in understanding marital satisfaction and explored the mediating role of mental health in establishing relationship between work-life balance and marital satisfaction.

Jang, Park and Zippay (2011) examined the relationship between employees' autonomy to control their work schedules, the availability of work-life programs, job satisfaction and mental health among 1,293 employees of 50 companies located in South Korea. By using multilevel analysis, they explored both individual and organization-level variables and examined the interaction effects of scheduling control and availability of work-life balance programs on job satisfaction and mental health. Results indicated that, the interaction effects of scheduling control and availability of work-life balance programs are positively related with job satisfaction and mental health. Further, the effect of scheduling control on job satisfaction and mental health was stronger when there was a availability of work-life balance programs, and job satisfaction mediates the effect of schedule control on mental health. These findings signified the importance of availability of work-life balance programs in the organizations, as family friendly organizations are perceived as more supportive for the employees, which enhances their job satisfaction, and eventually promotes mental health. In context of gender, the results were in the line of previous research as women were reporting significantly less job satisfaction and more mental stress than their counter part men.

Wang Li (2006) investigated the relationship between levels of perceived work stress, imbalance between work and family/personal lives and current depressive and anxiety disorders in 36,984 working population in Canada. Data from Canadian Community Health Survey for Mental health & Well-being (CCHS-1.2) were used for the study. Results indicated that the one month prevalence of mood and anxiety disorders was 3.6% and 4.0% for those who reported work stress score at 75th percentile and above. Further, those who reported that their work and family lives were "never" balanced, their one month prevalence of mood and anxiety disorders were 21.2% and 17.9%. The multivariate analyses showed that the work stress and imbalance between work and family/personal lives were independently associated with mood and anxiety disorders. Females were more associated with anxiety disorders, but no major depressive and mood disorders were reported. The study concluded that, work stress and imbalance between work and family/personals lives effect the mental condition of working population and imbalance between work and family/personal lives predict mental disorders strongly than work stress.

On the basis of above studies, we can conclude that work-life balance plays an important role in shaping the mental health of working population. Hence, it can be assumed that work-life balance will be related to the mental health of women managers.

2.3. Emotional Intelligence: Evolution of the concept

The term "Emotional Intelligence" emerged during mid-twentieth century, when the concept of emotional intelligence had been used in relation to psychotherapy treatments (Leuner, 1966) and to promoting personal and social well-being in general (Beasley 1987; Payne, 1986).

During 1980s, psychologists expressed their idea of multiple intelligence in which they conceptualized "emotional intelligence (EI)" as different form of human ability in context of emotions, apart from cognitive skills and intelligence (Gardner 1983; Sternberg 1985). Soon, the idea started appearing in scientific research and articles. Salovey & Mayer (1990) published an article entitled "Emotional Intelligence" which created great interest in the idea by the scientific community. They coined the term "Emotional Intelligence" and defined as "the ability to accurately perceive, evaluate and express emotions; the ability to have access to and/or to generate feelings which make thinking easier; the ability to understand emotions and emotional knowledge, and the ability to manage emotions by promoting emotional and intellectual growth" (Mayer & Salovey, 1997). The concept of EI got popularized by the book entitled "Emotional Intelligence: Why it can matter more than IQ" by Goleman (1995) and developed dramatically throughout late 1990s. Goleman (1995) defined Emotional Intelligence as "the ability to identify, assess, and control one's own emotions, the emotions of others, and that of groups". He argued that, our concept of human intelligence so far is too narrow, ignoring a critical part human ability (EI), which is very crucial for our success in personal and professional life. On the basis of brain and behavioral research, he explained the role of emotional intelligence in dealing with real-life challenges and situations. The differentiating role of emotional intelligence makes a person of average intelligence (IQ) more successful and valued at workplace than a person with high intelligence (IQ). A person with high emotional intelligence shows self-awareness, self-motivation, empathy, impulse control persistence and social deftness, which helps him/her excel in life and become successful at work place. Goleman further argued that, Emotional intelligence is not a fixed ability at birth; it can be learned and nurtured throughout the human life.

2.3.1. Emotional Intelligence: Important models

Researchers explained the concept of Emotional Intelligence under three different approaches: Trait approach, ability approach and mixed approach. Some consider EI as a human trait, while others consider it as an ability to learn and nurture throughout the life and some have mixed opinion regarding the concept. The important models under the three approaches are as follows:

A. The Trait EI model

The trait model of emotional intelligent is proposed by Petrides et al. (2001), derived from emotional self-efficacy theory. Trait EI model explains emotional intelligence as "Individual's self-perceptions of his/her emotional abilities". It considers emotional intelligence as innate human trait which is consistent with individual differences of one's personality. It concerns with people's perceptions of their emotional world, which can be measured through self-reporting questionnaires.

B. Mayer-Salovey (1997) ability model

It is also called as "four branch model" of emotional intelligence. According to this model emotional intelligence encompasses four types of abilities:

a) **Perceiving emotions:** It is the ability to recognize and interpret one's own emotions and express it correctly. It also includes identifying emotions through faces, voices and pictures.

b) **Using emotions:** It is the ability to use emotions to facilitate actions and achieve desired goals. An emotionally intelligent person uses his/her emotions in thinking, problem solving and decision making process wisely irrespective of the his/her present mood.

c) **Understanding emotions:** It is the ability to understand complex form of emotions and to recognize the transition of emotions from one state to another state. For example transition of emotions from happiness to anger or contentment to dissatisfaction etc.

d) **Managing emotions:** It is the ability to regulate one's own emotions as well as others in a productive way to achieve desired goals. To manage emotions properly one should be open to both positive and negative emotions and should have ability to connect and detach from the present state of emotion to act intelligently.

C. Goleman's Competency Model

Goleman's (1998) in his first model of emotional intelligence identified five dimensions of emotional intelligence encompassing twenty-five competencies. Three dimensions; self-awareness, motivation and self-regulations are related to personal competencies, which refers to the ability to identify and regulate one's own emotions. The remaining two dimensions; empathy and social skills refer to social competencies, which are related to understanding and regulating other's emotions. Later, Goleman (2000) refined his old model and proposed a new competency model which included four EI constructs;

a) **Self-awareness:** It is the ability to identify and understand one's own emotions to guide decisions.

b) **Self-management:** It is the ability to control and regulate one's own emotions to adapt and behave properly in response to changing circumstances.

c) **Social awareness:** It is the ability to sense and understand other's emotions while dealing with social networks and react accordingly.

d) **Relationship management:** It is the ability to influence, inspire and motivate others to develop healthy relationships and managing conflicts.

D. Bar-On Mixed model of EI

Reuven Bar-On (2006) developed the first tool for measuring emotional intelligence and used the term "Emotional Quotient". He opined that emotional intelligence has potential for performance and success. It develops over the period of time and can be enhanced through proper training and development programs.

The Bar-On model of EI includes five dimensions; intrapersonal, interpersonal, adaptability, stress management and general mood. Each dimension has sub-dimensions (factors) as follows:

a) **Intra-personal** : Self-Awareness, Assertiveness, Independence, Self-Regard, Self-Actualization

b) **Inter-personal:** Empathy, Social responsibility, Interpersonal relationship

c) **Stress Management:** Stress tolerance, Impulse control

d) **Adaptability:** Reality testing, Flexibility, Problem solving

e) **General Mood:** Optimism, Happiness

2.3.2. Emotional Intelligence: As moderator

According to "Conservation of resource (COR)" theory individual differences can be considered as personal resources which have a potential to weaken the negative impacts in crisis situations. Literature shows that emotional intelligence positively influences the outcomes of wok-life balance with different psychological constructs.

For example, Gao, Shi, Niu and Wang (2012) examined the moderating role of emotional intelligence (EI) on the relationship of work-family conflict (WFC) and job satisfaction (JS). Study was conducted on 212 high school teachers in China, age ranging from 22 to 67 years (Mean =30.72 years). Moderation analysis was done through hierarchical multiple regression followed by simple slope analysis method. Results indicated that WFC (work-to-family interference and family-to-work interference) was negatively related to job satisfaction and that emotional intelligence weakened the effect of WFC on job satisfaction. Hence, EI had a moderation relationship with WFC and job satisfaction.

Ugoani (2013) examined the role of emotional intelligence in balancing work-family conflict among dual-career-parents in Nigeria. Data were collected from 476 respondents in Aba, Owerri and Umuahia, South-East Nigeria. Analysis was done through frequencies, percentages and Chi-square statistics. Results indicated that emotional intelligence is crucial for balancing work-family conflict among dual-career parents in Nigeria.

Lenaghan, Buda and Eisner (2007) examined the role of emotional intelligence with work-family conflict and well-being of 205 US employees. Majority of respondents were married females. Age of the respondents ranged between 19 to 70 years (Mean=47.48 years). Analysis of the data was done through correlations and multiple regression analysis. Results indicated that emotional intelligence is positively correlated with well-being and act as protector (moderator) variable in the impact of work-family conflict and well-being of employees. Respondents having higher emotional intelligence with low work-family conflict reported higher well-being in compare to respondents having low emotional intelligence and high work-family conflict. Thus, emotional intelligence played a moderating role on the relationship of work-family conflict and well-being of employees.

Gupta and Kumar (2010) investigated the relationship of emotional intelligence with self-efficacy and mental health of college students in India. Data were collected from 200 college students (100 males & 100 females) of Kurukshetra University, India. Analysis of data was done through correlation and t-test analysis. Results revealed that, emotional intelligence is positively correlated with self-efficacy and mental health of participants and male students reported better than female students in terms of emotional intelligence, self-efficacy and mental health. Results indicated the importance of training programs and interventions to improve the emotional intelligence, self-efficacy and mental health of female students in India.

On the basis of above studies, we can conclude that emotional intelligence plays an important role in balancing work and family life and also influences individual's mental health. Hence it can be assumed that, emotional intelligence would have a moderating role on the relationship of work-life balance and mental health of women managers in Indian work-family culture.

2.4. Personality: Evolution of the concept

The term personality has been originated from the Latin word "Persona" which means mask. Ancient time, in Greece and Rome theatre artist used to wear mask to play certain characters. Thus, personality is used in terms of influencing others through external appearance. But, scientists have defined personality in much broader term as "personality is the dynamic organization within the individual of those psychophysical systems that determine his unique adjustment to the environment" (Allport, 1937).

The above definition clearly indicates that personality is dynamic in its nature and is always changing. It is not static. Allport also suggested that personality is an integrating and organizing agent between physiological (of the body) and psychological (of the mind) aspects of an individual. It is unique in nature. It becomes habitual to the person. It results in action or behavior in relation to a person, organization or situation. Allport's landmark book "Personality: A Psychological Interpretation" is considered as formal beginning of the study of personality. He identified almost fifty definitions of personality and classified them into five different categories as follows:

1) **Omnibus:** These definitions view personality as the sum-total, aggregate or constellation of properties or qualities.

2) **Integrative and configurational:** Under this view of personality, the organization of personal attributes is stressed.

3) **Hierarchical:** These definitions specify the various levels of integration or organization of personality.

4) **Adjustment:** This view emphasizes the adjustment (adaptation, survival and evolution) of the person to the environment.

5) **Distinctiveness:** The definitions for this category stress uniqueness of each personality.

Following the Allport's effort, other books and journals on personality started appearing in educational industry. Later, courses in Personality started in universities and research undertaken. These activities triggered the fact that, some areas concern to psychoanalysts and neo-psychoanalysts could be merged into psychology. Academic psychologists started believing that there is a possibility to develop a scientific study of personality. From 1930s to present date, a variety of approaches to the study of personality have emerged (Schultz & Schultz, 2012).

2.4.1. Personality: Important theories

There are numerous theories exist in literature of personality, which falls under different approaches of studying personality. Each approach describes different patterns in personality and explains how these patters define one's personality different from others. The important approaches and underlying theories of personality are as follows:

A. The Psychoanalytic approach

Sigmund Freud, the pioneer of this approach believed that the early childhood events, the unconscious mind and sexual instincts play an important role in formation and development of one's personality.

Freud's earlier conception divided personality into three levels: conscious, pre-conscious and unconscious. As defined by Freud, the conscious part includes all the sensations and experiences of which one is aware of at any point of time. It is the limited aspect of personality in which thoughts, sensations and memories exist in conscious state at any time. The unconscious part contains the major driving power behind all behaviors. It is the repository of instincts, wishes and desires which we cannot see or control but they direct our behavior. Between conscious and unconscious the third level is pre-conscious. It is the storehouse of perceptions, memories, and thoughts of which we are not conscious at a given time, but we can easily summon into conscious mind.

Freud later revised this notion of three levels of personality and proposed three basic parts in the structure of personality: the id, the ego and the superego. The id is the primary part of personality which runs on instincts and desires. It operates on pleasure principle irrespective of what other people wants. The ego is the second part of personality which is rational in nature. It fulfills the desires of id through realistic ways and provides justification and rationalization of these desires. The superego is the part of personality which represents human's higher qualities. It works on moral framework and guides the behaviors of human being through sense of right and wrong.

B. The Neo-psychoanalytic approach

Under neo-psychoanalytic various personality theorists proposed their views on human personality which derived from Freudian psychoanalysis, but differs on certain issues.

Carl Jung offered a new and elaborated explanation of human personality which he called as **analytical psychology.** He believed that human personality can be classified into two categories:

1) Introverts- obtain energy from the "internal world" or from solitude with the self.
2) Extroverts- obtain energy from the "external worlds" or from the interactions with others.

Further, Jung identified four essential psychological functions which is experienced by both extroverts and introverts. These are: Thinking, feeling, sensation, intuition. These functions are more dominant than others in each person.

Jung's theory has a great impact on field of personality research. The popular self-reporting Myers-Briggs Type Indicator Test (MBIT) is best on Jung's theory of personality.

Alfred Alder explained personality as unique characteristic of each individual and denied the role of biological instincts and childhood experiences in developing personality as described by Sigmund Freud. He called his approach as **individual psychology**.

According to Adler, human is primarily a social being. Human personality is influenced and shaped by social environments and interactions. Adler minimized the role of sex and unconscious part of mind in defining one's personality, rather he emphasized conscious part as core of the personality which we can see and control. To Adler, it is the conscious part which actively involved in shaping our personality and guiding our future.

Karen Horney was another neo-psychoanalytic theorist, who presented views about personality different from Sigmund Freud. Like Adler, Horney placed greater emphasis on social relationships and interactions as factors of shaping human personality. She argued that biological factor (sex) is not the governing factor as explained by Freud. She challenged Freudian concept of Oedipus complex, the libido, and the three part structure of personality. According to Horney, human are motivated by sexual or aggressive forces but by the needs for security and love.

C. The Life-Span approach

Under this approach **Erik Erikson** proposed his **Identity theory** of personality. His work was an extension of Freud work but departed substantially from orthodox psychoanalytic theory. According to Freud personality is shaped by age of childhood (up to 5 years approximately), but Erikson suggested that personality continues to develop over the entire life span.

Erikson placed greater importance on the ego part than on the id. According to him, ego is not dependent on or subservient to the id, but it is an independent part of personality. He also emphasized on the role of cultural and historical forces in shaping human personality. He questioned the sole involvement of innate biological factors in formation of personality.

D. The Humanistic approach

The humanistic approach to personality is a part of the humanistic movement which flourished during 1960s to 1970s. Humanistic psychologists criticized Freud and other psychoanalysts for studying personality from emotionally disturbed side of human nature. It focused on positive characteristics like strengths and virtues of human nature to study personality at its best, not worst.

Abraham Maslow is considered as founder of humanistic psychology movement. He objected psychoanalysis and behaviorism and emphasized on positive human qualities to explain human behavior and personality.

Maslow proposed theory of "hierarchy of five innate needs" that activate and guide human behavior. Following the hierarchy these needs are: physiological needs, safety needs, love and belongingness needs, According to Maslow, these needs are instinctual in nature which carry hereditary component but may influenced by social expectations, learning and fear of disapproval. The needs are arranged in order from lower needs to higher needs. Lower needs must be fulfilled before higher needs become activated. For example, a hungry person feels no urge for esteem needs. When he gets adequate food to satisfy his hunger then only he can seek approval and esteem from other people.

The theory of Maslow is not derived from case histories of clinical patients but from study on creative, independent, fulfilled and self-sufficient adults. From his research he concluded that human beings are born with same set of instinctual needs which enable them to develop, grow and reach their full potential.

Carl Rogers proposed his personality theory as framework for the patient-therapist relationship, rooted in humanistic psychology. He believed that humans are rational beings rules by their conscious perception of selves and outer world. He questioned the role of unconscious and other factors of Freudian psychoanalysis. He rejected the role of past events as controlling force to influence the present behavior, rather he emphasized that, current feelings and emotions have greater impact on human personality. However, he recognized that the childhood events influence the way one perceive outer environment and self. Since, the emphasis was on the present and conscious part; Rogers argue that personality can be understood from one's own view point based on his/her subjective experiences.

Rogers's personality theory was not based on experimental laboratory research but, on his experiences with his clients, which is driven from therapeutic approach. Hence it has great relevance in today's counseling situations.

E. Trait approach

The trait approach focuses on identifying, describing and measuring specific traits in human being which defines human personality. The combination and interaction of these traits make each personality different from others. Different theorists have proposed different number of traits which make up the human personality.

Gordon Allport categorized personality traits into three levels:

1. **Cardinal traits:** It is the pervasive and influential trait in human which touches every aspect of life. It is a kind of strong passion and powerful force which dominates and guide behavior. For example; chauvinism, narcissism etc.

2. **Central traits:** These are the traits which we use to describe someone's personality. They form the basic foundation of personality, some 5 to 10 characteristics, which best describe the person's behavior. For example; intelligent, honest, shy etc.

3. **Secondary traits:** These are the less influential traits which appear only in certain situations or under certain circumstances. These are generally related to attitudes and preferences. For example; getting anxious while addressing a group of people.

Hans Eysenck, a british psychologist developed a personality model based on three universal traits. These are:

1. **Introversion/ Extraversion:** Introvert persons direct their attention to inner experiences, while extrovert persons direct their attention on other peoples and outer environment. In general, a person high in introversion are tend to be quiet and reserved, while a person in high extraversion are sociable and outgoing.

2. **Neuroticism/Emotional stability:** Neuroticism refers to instability of emotions, causing an individual to become emotionally upset.

Emotional stability refers to the tendency to remain emotionally constant or stable.

3. **Psychoticism:** Eysenck added this dimension to his earlier model after studying mentally ill people. Individuals high on this trait are tend to hostile, anti-social, non-empathetic and they face difficulty in dealing with reality.

Leading to personality research **Robert McCrae and Paul Costa** proposed their "Big Five Theory of personality". It is considered as robust model to explain human personality. According to this theory, five core traits are present in every individual at varying degree which defines their personality. These traits are:

1. **Extraversion**

2. **Agreeableness**

3. **Conscientiousness**

4. **Neuroticism**

5. **Openness**

The combination of these five traits at varying degree in human personality makes each people unique and different from each other.

2.4.2. Personality: As moderator

Despite important advancement in work-family literature, role of personality characteristics in balancing work and family life has been less studied (Sumer & Knight,

2001). Few studies have acknowledged the relationship of personality characteristics and work-life balance and its impact on work outcomes and individuals mental health.

Ghorpade, Lackritz and Singh (2011) investigated the moderating role of personality on the relationship between role conflict, role ambiguity and burnout (emotional exhaustion, depersonalization and personal accomplishment) on sample of 263 faculty members at state university, California. Analysis strategy included descriptive, correlation and stepwise regression analysis. Results revealed that, role conflict was related with greater emotional exhaustion, while extraversion and emotional stability was related with reduced emotional exhaustion. Role conflict was related with increased depersonalization, while agreeableness decreased depersonalization. Role ambiguity was related with decreased personal accomplishments, while agreeableness and emotional stability increased personal accomplishments. Further, extraversion moderated the relationship between role conflict and personal accomplishments, while conscientiousness moderated the relationship between role ambiguity and personal accomplishments.

Wayne, Musisca and Fleeson (2004) investigated the relationship of Big five personality traits with conflict and facilitation between work and family roles and also examined the impact of conflict and facilitation on job and family effort and satisfaction. Data was taken from national random sample (N=2130) and analysis was done through descriptive, correlation and multiple regression analysis. Results revealed that extraversion was positively related with work-family facilitation, but not related with conflict between the roles. Neuroticism was strongly related with conflict but weakly related with facilitation.

Conscientiousness was found negatively related with work-family conflict. Further, facilitation was found positively related with work-family outcomes i.e. lower job and family efforts and satisfaction, whereas conflict was found negatively related with the same outcomes. The study emphasized on the knowledge of individual personality traits to reduce conflict, enhance facilitation and maximize the positive outcomes of work and family roles.

Kinnunen, Vermulst, Gerris and Makikangas (2003) examined the moderating role of personality on the relationship between work-family conflict and well being of 296 full-time employed fathers in Netherland. Data analysis was done through hierarchical multiple regression analysis. Results indicated that, emotional stability moderated the relationship work interference with family (WIF) and job exhaustion and between WIF and depression. Further, agreeableness moderated the relationship between family interference with work (FIW) and marital satisfaction. Besides the moderating effects, both WIF and FIW and emotional stability and agreeableness had main effect on well being of respondents.

Senf and Liau (2013) examined the moderating role of personality on the effect of gratitude and strengths based interventions on happiness and depressive symptoms of 122 participants. Data were collected at three stages: baseline, post-intervention assessment and 1-month follow up assessment. The findings of the study partially supported the effectiveness of the gratitude and strengths-based interventions in enhancing happiness and reducing depressive symptoms compared to control group. In addition it was also found that extraversion has moderating effect on gratitude-based intervention on happiness and openness showed positive moderating role alongside extraversion on effect of interventions on post-intervention happiness.

On the basis of above studies we can conclude that personality traits have influence on individual's work-life balance and mental health. Hence it can be assumed that personality would have moderating effect on work-life balance and mental health of women managers.

2.5. Theoretical Framework

2.5.1. Conservation of Resource theory (COR)

The present work is based on "Conservation of resource (COR)" theory proposed by Hobfoll (1989). It is one of the leading theories in organizational psychology relevant to predicting people's behavior and cognition in different life domains and at different institutional settings.

According to conservation of resource theory, people want to retain, protect and maintain their resources which they centrally value. It classifies resources broadly in four categories: personal, material, condition, and energy resources. Material resources include house, vehicle, furniture etc., Condition resources include job profile, marital status etc. Energies include time, knowledge, skills etc. while, personal resources include, physical health, type of personality, ability to regulate emotions etc. Resources may be at outside the self (contextual) or within the self (personal) and may be volatile and durable (Hobfoll, 2002; Brummelhuis & Bakker, 2012). Stress occurs a) when key or central resources are threatened with loss b) when key or central resources are lost or c) when after significant effort individual is unable to gain key or central resources.

2.5.2 Principles of Conservation of resources (COR) theory

COR theory is basically a motivational theory which explains much about human behavior based on evolutionary need to acquire, retain and conserve resources for survival which is central to human nature. Like any other theory, COR theory is also based on certain principles which are explained below:

1. The first principle of COR theory is that resource loss is disproportionately more salient than resource gain. In compare to resource gain, resource loss has greater impact, high momentum with longer duration. Resource loss tends to affect people more rapidly with increasing speed over time. The probable reason behind this as people are products of evolution and in evolutionary terms even small loss of key resources significantly related to failure to survive.

2. The second principle of COR theory is that people must invest resources in order to gain resources, recover from lost resources and protect against loss of resources. It includes direct replacement of resources, such as using saving at the time of income loss and indirect investment of resources such as increasing savings to prepare for tough financial situation.

3. The third principle of COR theory states that resource gain increases in salience in the context of resource loss (Hobfoll et al. 2018). It means, when the circumstances of resource loss are high, resource gain become more important as it gains value.

4. The fourth principle of COR theory is that when resources are exhausted or outstretched, people enter into defensive mode to preserve the self. They may become aggressive and sometimes irrational. This is likely to be built-in evolutionary strategy adopted by the person to become defensive (i.e., conservation of resources) or exploratory (i.e., search for alternate adaptation or survival strategy for coping the stressful situation). This is the least researched principle of COR theory but has high explanatory power.

2.5.3. Corollaries of Conservation of resources (COR) theory

COR theory proposes certain key corollaries. Like principles, these corollaries also make specific and multifaceted predictions about adopting complex strategies required to cope up with stressful events at the individual and organizational level.

1. Corollary first states that resource loss and gain both are integral to vulnerability and resilience. People or organizations with greater resources are less vulnerable to resource loss and more capable of resource gain, whereas people or organization with lack of resources is more vulnerable to resource loss and less capable of resource gain.

2. Corollary second states that resource loss has spiraling nature. As people having fewer resources are vulnerable to further resource loss, it forms a "spiral loss".With each iteration of the spiral loss people have fewer resources to replace the resource loss. The impact is more powerful in case of resource loss than resource gain.

3. Corollary third states that resource gain has also spiraling nature, but since resource gain is less impactful, the cycle is slower than resource loss. People who gain resources are better able to obtain other resources that is, resources generate additional resources, which forms a "spiral gain", but the cycle is weaker in compare to spiral loss and take time to develop.

2.5.4. Resource Caravans and Resource Caravan Passageways

COR theory develops a greater understanding on interrelationship between resources and how contexts and environment provide favorable or unfavorable conditions to create, maintain and limit the resources. It contrasts the general notion of static nature of resources.

1. **Resource caravans:** According to Hobfoll (2011a), resources do not exist individually rather travel in caravans or packs for both individuals and organizations. Since, resources develop due to learned adaptation and nurturance; they are likely to be co-travelers. For example, self-efficacy, self-esteem and optimism generate from common fertile environment and developmental conditions, hence they are highly correlated and travel in caravans.

2. **Resource caravan passageways:** According to the COR theory, resources exist, nurture or limit in particular environment and conditions. The organization, culture, allowances and facilitations i.e. the passageways have major role in creating, maintaining and fostering the resources. Hence, while studying and analyzing the resources one should acquire a broader view including the social

and ecological environment of organization apart from considering only the individual level.

2.5.5. Theoretical model

From the perspective of conservation of resources theory (COR), we are assuming emotional intelligence and personality as personal resources, which have potential to moderate the relationship between work life balance and mental health of women managers. The conceptual diagram is shown in Fig. 2.1.

Figure 2.1. Conceptual diagram (model)

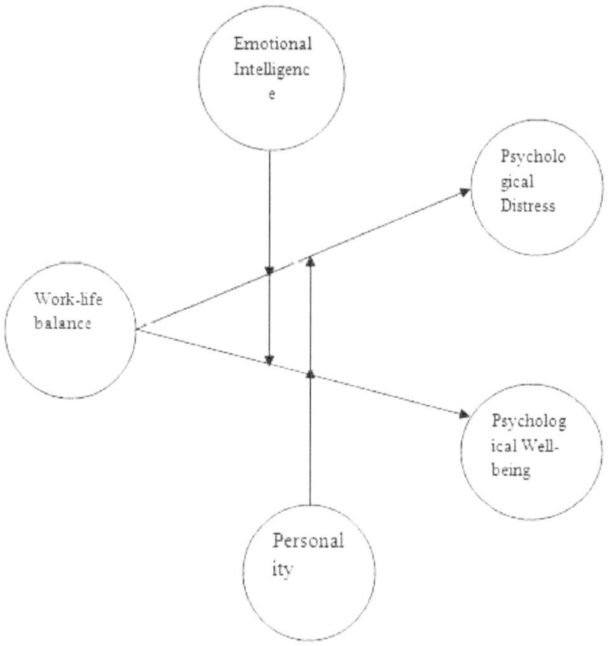

On the basis of hypothesized model following objectives of the study are formulated:

1. To study and compare work-life balance (work interference with personal life, personal life interference with work, work-personal life enhancement), mental health (psychological distress and psychological wellbeing), emotional intelligence (self-emotion appraisal, others' emotion appraisal, use of emotions, regulation of emotion) and personality (extraversion, openness, agreeableness, conscientiousness and neuroticism) of women managers working in public and private sector organizations.

2. To study the relationship between the dimensions of work-life balance, mental health, emotional intelligence and personality of women managers.

3. To examine the moderating role of emotional intelligence on the relationship of work-life balance and psychological distress of women managers.

4. To examine the moderating role of emotional intelligence on the relationship of work-life balance and psychological wellbeing of women managers.

5. To examine the moderating role of each dimensions of personality (extraversion, openness, agreeableness, conscientiousness and neuroticism) on the relationship of work-life balance and psychological distress of women managers.

6. To examine the moderating role of each dimensions of personality (extraversion, openness, agreeableness, conscientiousness and neuroticism) on the relationship of work-life balance and psychological well-being of women managers.

On the basis of objectives of the study following hypotheses are formulated:

H1: There would be a significant difference between women managers working in government and private sector organizations on the dimension of work-life balance (work interference with personal life, personal life interference with work, work-personal life enhancement), mental health (psychological distress and psychological wellbeing), emotional intelligence (self-emotion appraisal, others' emotion appraisal, use of emotions, regulation of emotion) and personality (extraversion, openness, agreeableness, conscientiousness and neuroticism).

H2: There would be a significant relationship between dimensions of work-life balance, mental health, emotional intelligence and personality of women managers.

H3: There would be a moderating effect of emotional intelligence on the relationship of work-life balance and psychological distress of women managers.

H4: There would be a moderating effect of emotional intelligence on the relationship of work-life balance and psychological wellbeing of women managers.

H5: There would be a moderating effect of each dimensions of personality (extraversion, agreeableness, conscientiousness and neuroticism) on the relationship of work-life balance and psychological distress of women managers.

H6: There would be a moderating effect of each dimensions of personality (extraversion, openness, agreeableness, conscientiousness and neuroticism) on the relationship of work-life balance and psychological wellbeing of women managers

3.1. Research Design

To study the research problem, a mixed method research design (**Convergent design,** Wittink, et al. 2006) has been adopted, in which both quantitative as well as qualitative analyses have been done in parallel and results were interpreted to draw some conclusion.

In quantitative section, hypotheses have been formulated through literature review and theoretical framework. To test the hypotheses, data have been collected through valid standardized tools. After collecting data, appropriate statistical techniques have been used to analyze the data to draw results.

In qualitative section, research questions have been developed through literature review and study of the population. Face-to-face interviews have been taken from the respondents to gather relevant qualitative data. Interpretive Phenomenological Analysis (IPA) has been used to analyze qualitative data to answer research questions.

3.2. Participants and Procedure

For quantitative analysis, total 311 women managers were randomly chosen from different organizations of Delhi and National Capital Region (NCR) in India. A formal consent was taken before administering the tests on the participants. Total 500 questionnaires were distributed, on which 343 were returned (response rate =68.6%). After removing the partially filled questionnaires and outliers, total 311 participants (158 from public sector organizations & 153 from private sector organizations) were included in the study. The average age of the participants was 34.08 (SD=8.6) years.

To alleviate the effect of **"common method biases"** appropriate procedural and statistical steps are taken into account. First, we counterbalanced the order of measurement of independent and dependent variables in such a way that 60 items of two moderator variables were entirely separating the independent and dependent variables in the questionnaire. It helped in controlling "priming effects, item-context-mood states, and other biases related to question context". (Podsakoff et. al., 2003). Second, we ensured respondent anonymity to check leniency, social desirability and consistency bias (Podsakoff et al. 2003). Third, to identify common method variance, we conducted Harman's single factor test. It was found that the first single factor accounted only 20.8% of variance, which is much below than 50% hence, there was no significant amount of common method variance present in the data (Podsakoff et al., 2003; Podsakoff & Organ, 1986).

3.3. Measures

3.3.1. Socio-demographic Data Sheet: A self made semi-structure data sheet was used to collect information regarding the demographic variables like age, educational qualification, designation, type of organization, marital status, duration of marriage, number of children, number of dependent elders, type of family, distance of workplace from the residence, and income (per month) of the participants.

3.3.2. Work-life balance Scale (Hayman, 2005): To assess work-life balance of women managers, work-life balance scale developed by Hayman (2005) has been used. The scale consisted of 15 items, which measures three dimensions of work-life balance: "work interference with personal life (WIPL-7 items), personal life interference with work (PLIW-4 items) and work/personal life enhancement (WPLE- 4 items)". The participants were asked to indicate the frequency with which they felt in a particular way during the past three months about their work-life balance. Responses were measured on seven point scale (1= Not at all, 4= Sometimes & 7= All the time). Reliability of the scale estimated using Cronbach alpha coefficient in the present sample is 0.875 for WIPL, 0.784 for PLIW and 0.840 for WPLE. Empirical evidence of higher order confirmatory factor analysis showed that the three dimensions make work-life balance (WLB) a higher order construct (Fisher-McAuley, et al., 2003). The Cronbach alpha coefficient of the scale for the present sample is found to be 0.770.

3.3.3. Emotional Intelligence Scale (Wong & Law, 2002). To assess the emotional intelligence of managers Emotional Intelligence scale developed by Wong and Law (2002) has been used. The scale consisted of 16 items which measures four dimensions of Emotional Intelligence: "Self emotional appraisal (SEA-4 items), Others' emotional appraisal (OEA- 4 items), Regulation of emotion (ROE) and Use of emotion (UOE-4 items)". Participants were asked to describe their emotional intelligence on seven point scale (1= Strongly disagree, 4= Neither agree nor disagree & 7= Strongly agree). The Cronbach alpha coefficient in the present sample is 0.853 for SEA, 0.848 for OEA and 0.882 for UOE and 0.883 for ROE. Empirical evidence of higher order confirmatory factor analysis showed that the four dimensions make Emotional intelligence (EI) a higher order construct (Wong & Law, 2002). The Cronbach alpha coefficient for the scale is found to be 0.913.

3.3.4. Big Five Inventory (John & Srivastava, 1999). To measure the personality characteristics of women managers Big Five Inventory (BFI) developed by O.P. John and S. Srivastava (1999) has been used. The inventory consists of 44-items, which measures an individual on the Big Five Factors (dimensions) of personality (Goldberg, 1993). These dimensions are: Extraversion (8-items), Agreeableness (9-items),

Conscientiousness (9-items), Neuroticism (8-items) and Openness (10-items). Each of the dimensions is then further divided into personality facets.

Participants were asked to response on number of statements that may or may not apply to them. They had to rate each statements on five point Likert scale (1= Disagree strongly, 3= neither agree nor disagree, 5= Agree strongly). The Cronbach alpha coefficient in the present sample is 0.694 for Extraversion, 0.747 for Agreeableness, 0.735 for Conscientiousness, 0.727 for Neuroticism and 0.748 for Openness.

3.3.5. Mental Health Inventory-38 (Veit & Ware, 1983): To assess mental health of managers the Mental Health Inventory-38 (Veit & Ware, 1983) has been used. The inventory consisted of 38 items, which measures multidimensional nature of psychological well-being and psychological distress including: anxiety, depression, loss of behavioral/emotional control, general positive affect, emotional ties and life satisfaction. All of the 38 items are scored on a six-point scale ranging 1 to 6, except two items (9 & 28) are scored on a five-point scale ranging 1to5.

The MHI-38 can be aggregated into six subscales: "Anxiety, Depression, Loss of Behavioral/Emotional Control, General positive effect, Emotional ties and Life satisfaction, two global scales: Psychological Distress and Psychological Well-being and a global Mental Health Index score". In the present study we have used two global scales i.e. Psychological well-being and Psychological distress for data analysis as higher order confirmatory factor analysis of present sample showed that the two factors, psychological well-being and psychological distress do not make mental health a composite construct. The Cronbach alpha in the present sample is 0.920 for Psychological wellbeing, 0.946 for Psychological distress.

4.1. Tools used in Data collection

There were four measures used for data collection:

a) Work-life balance scale (Hayman, 2005) -15 items

b) Emotional Intelligence Scale (Wong &Law, 2002)- 16 items

c) Big Five Inventory (John & Srivastava, 1999)- 44 items

d) Mental Health Inventory (Veit & Ware, 1983)-38 items

Since all these measures were western in origin, they have been validated for the current Indian sample. To validate the tools adequate sample has been collected and after data collection tools are validated one by one through Confirmatory Factor Analysis (CFA).

4.2. Sample

To validate the tools total 500 questionnaires were distributed among the women managers working in organizations of Delhi and NCR, on which 343 were returned (response rate=68.6%). After removing partially filled questionnaires and outliers, total 311 participants were considered for the study.

 Confirmatory Factor Analysis requires the application of Structural Equation Modeling (SEM), in which a minimum sample size is required. According to Hair et.al. (2018), models with seven constructs or less, with modest communalities (0.5) and no under-identified (less than three items) constructs , at least 150 sample size is required for model to be estimated. However, to perform different model fit indices accurately for demonstrating Goodness-of-Fit, more than 250 sample is required for constructs having more than 30 items (Hair, et.al., 2018).

Since we have sample of 311 participants, and none of the constructs is under-identified, the sample size is adequate to run Confirmatory Factor Analysis for each measure.

4.3. Procedure

To conduct Confirmatory Factor Analysis, data were entered into software IBM SPSS 21. Then the data file was uploaded into software IBM AMOS 21. Path model was drawn for each measure on AMOS software to demonstrate the relationship between observed variables (items) and latent construct. After completing each path in the model and putting required constraints, each model was estimated to test how well the measured variables (items) represents the construct. Further to test the validity of constructs, model fit indices were checked for their optimum values and accordingly items were deleted or retained to obtain best model-fit for the constructs.

4.4. Work-life balance Scale (Hayman, 2005)

Confirmatory factor analysis was done on Work-life balance scale to test its proposed three-factor structure. The scale consists of 15 items, which measures three dimensions of work-life balance:

a) Work interference with personal life (WIPL)- 7 items

b) Personal life interference with work (PLIW)- 4 items

c) Work/personal life enhancement (WPLE)- 4 items

First order confirmatory analysis was run to see factor loadings of the items and correlation among the three dimensions. Some widely accepted model fit indices including GFI, AGFI, NFI, TLI, CFI, RMSEA and SRMR were also checked within their permissible limit to determine model fit. The recommended values for these fit indices guided the acceptability and fitness of the model (Hair et.al. 2018).

The first order confirmatory factor analysis of work-life balance scale is shown in figure below:

Figure 4.1. First order CFA of work-life balance scale

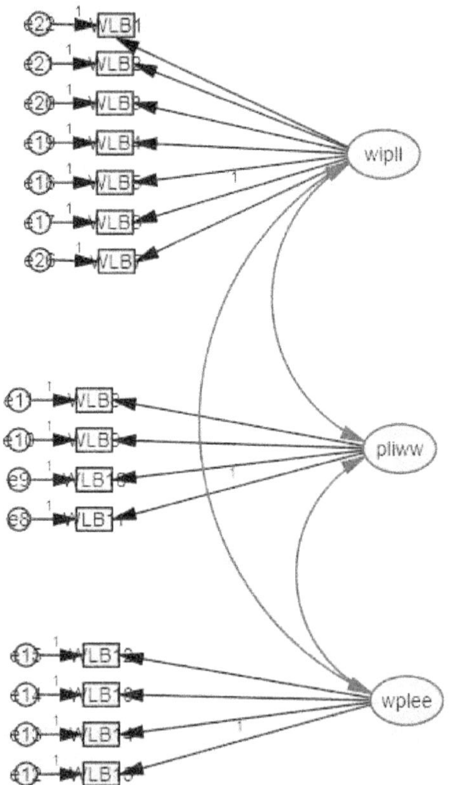

Table 4.1. Fit indices of the original work-life balance scale and the modified version on current sample (First order CFA)

Model Fit Indices	Model 1 (original)	Model 2 Removed item no. 7
CMIN	283.684	262.402
Df	87	74
P	<0.001	<0.001
CMIN/df	3.261	3.546
GFI	0.891	0.892
AGFI	0.849	0.847
NFI	0.880	0.887
TLI	0.895	0.896
CFI	0.913	0.915
RMSEA	0.085	0.091
SRMR	.0586	.0575
CHI SQUARE DIFFERENCE TEST		X2diff=21.282 p >0.05

Table .4.1 shows results of first order CFA of work-life balance scale. It includes the fit indices of original Work-life balance scale and the modified version of the scale on the current sample. After conducting CFA on original work-life balance scale, factor loadings of the all items were checked. Among all items, item number 7 had lowest factor loading (0.273), so the item 7 was removed to get better model fit. After removing item 7, model fit indices were checked for model 2, but there was no improvement in the model 2. Values of AGFI and NFI have decreased and values of Normed Chi-square (CMIN/df) and RMSEA have increased. In addition, chi-square difference test was also found to be insignificant for the model 2 (X^2 diff= 21.28, p> 0.05). Therefore, model 1 (original scale) has been accepted as better model and item 7 has been retained in the scale.

4.4.1. Work-life balance as a Higher Order Construct

Empirical evidence shows that the three dimensions of work-life balance (work interference with personal life, personal life interference with work and work/personal life enhancement) make work-life balance a higher order construct (Fisher-McAuley, et al., 2003). To test how well the three dimensions represents work-life balance as a higher order construct, second order CFA was run on the data again using AMOS software.

Figure 4.2 represents the structure of work-life balance as a higher order construct consisting three first order constructs. As shown in figure paths were drawn from composite construct work-life balance to three dimensions of work-life balance. The whole structure represents work-life balance scale as higher order reflective measure.

Figure 4.2. The second order CFA model of Work-life balance Scale

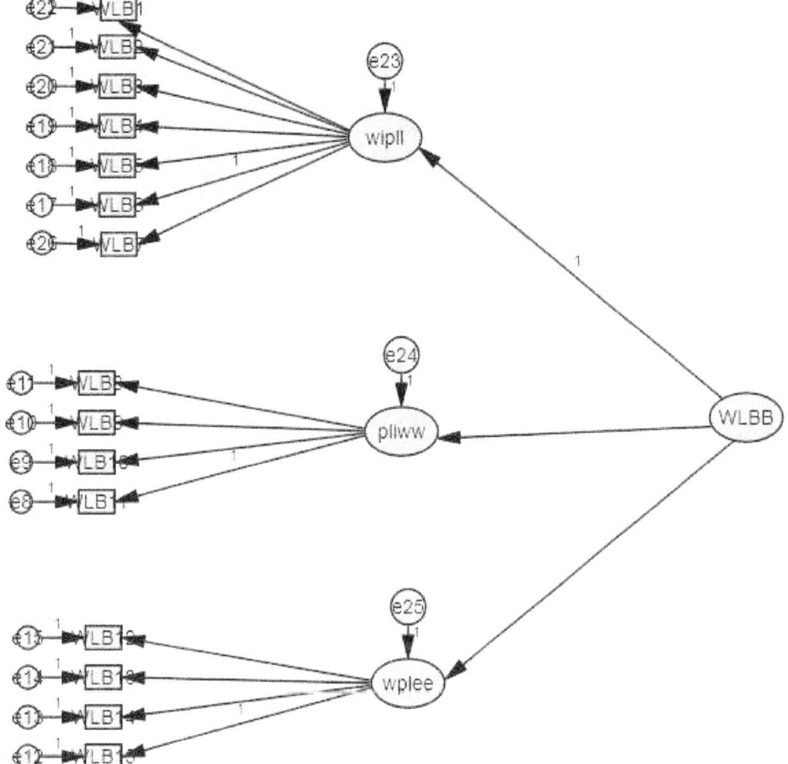

Table 4.2. Second order CFA Fit indices for Work-life balance Scale

Model Fit Indices	Model 1	Model 2 Item no.7 deleted
CMIN	283.684	262.402
df	87	74
P	<0.001	<0.001
CMIN/df	3.261	3.546
GFI	0.891	0.892
AGFI	0.849	0.847
NFI	0.880	0.887
TLI	0.895	0.896
CFI	0.913	0.915
RMSEA	0.08	0.091
SRMR	0.058	0.057
CHI SQUARE DIFFERENCE TEST		X2diff=21.282 p>0.05

Table 4.2 shows the model fit indices of second order CFA of work-life balance scale. As we can see in model 1, the value of GFI, TLI, CFI, RMSEA and SRMR are within their permissible range for good model fit and chi-square is also significant at 0.001 level, it can be concluded that the three dimensions work-interference with personal life, personal life interference with work and work/personal life enhancement reflect a larger theme of work-life balance. This model represents a hierarchical structure of work-life balance, in which the three dimensions compositely represent an underlying latent construct of work-life balance.

As in the model 1, the factor loading of item 7 was lowest, we checked an additional model after deleting item 7(model 2), but after deleting the item model did not show significant improvements. The values of CMIN/df and RMSEA has increased and chi-square difference test was also found to be insignificant (X^2 diff= 21.28, p>0.05). Therefore model 1 is accepted as better model to represent work-life balance as a higher order construct.

Table 4.3. Factors, items and factor loadings of the final version of Work-life balance scale used in current study

Factor	Items	Factor loadings
Work interference with personal life	1. "Personal life suffers because of work"	0.810
	2. "Job makes personal life difficult"	0.825
	3. "Neglect personal needs because of work"	0.834
	4. "Put personal life on hold for work"	0.779
	5. "Miss personal activities because of work"	0.831
	6. "Struggle to juggle work and non-work"	0.676
	7. "Happy with the amount of time for non –work activities"	0.273
Personal life interference with work	8. "Personal life drains me of energy for work"	0.609
	9. "Too tired to be effective at work"	0.742
	10. "My work suffers because of my personal life"	0.722
	11. "Hard to work because of personal matters"	0.713

Work/Personal life enhancement	12. "Personal life gives me energy for my job"	0.779
	13. "Job gives me energy to pursue personal activities"	0.612
	14. "Better mood at work because of personal life"	0.902
	15. "Better mood because of my job"	0.699

4.5. Emotional Intelligence Scale (Wong & Law, 2002)

Confirmatory factor analysis was done on Emotional Intelligence Scale to test its proposed four-factor structure. The scale consists of 16 items, which measures four dimensions of emotional intelligence:

a) Self-emotion appraisal (SEA)- 4 items

b) Others' emotion appraisal (OEA)- 4 items

c) Use of emotion (UOE)- 4 items

d) Regulation of emotion (ROE)- 4 items

First order confirmatory analysis was run to see factor loadings of the items and correlation among the four dimensions. Some widely accepted model fit indices including CMIN/df, GFI, AGFI, NFI, TLI, CFI, RMSEA and SRMR were also checked within their permissible limit to determine model fit. The recommended values for these fit indices guided the acceptability and fitness of the model (Hair et.al. 2018).

The first order confirmatory factor analysis of emotional intelligence scale is shown in figure 4.3:

Figure 4.3. First order CFA of Emotional Intelligence scale

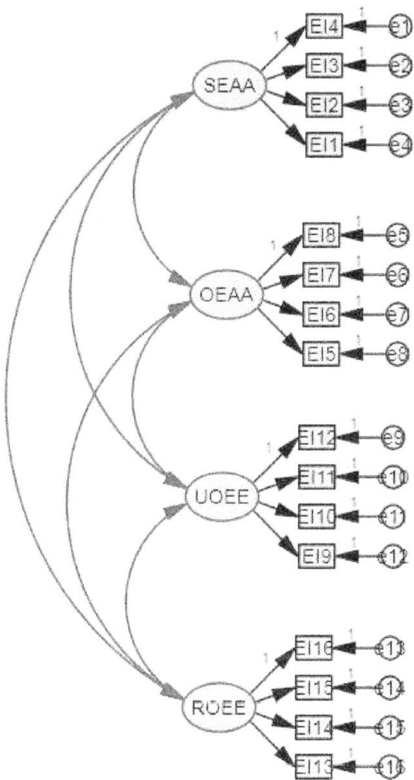

Table 4.4. Fit indices of the Emotional Intelligence Scale (First order CFA)

Model Fit Indices	Model 1 (original)
CMIN	180.214
df	98
p	<0.001
CMIN/df	1.839
GFI	0.933
AGFI	0.908
NFI	0.938
TLI	0.964
CFI	0.971
RMSEA	0.052
SRMR	0.0427

Table 4.4 shows results of first order CFA of Emotional Intelligence Scale. It includes the model fit indices of original scale on the current sample. Since, values of GFI, AGFI, NFI, TLI and CFI are more than 0.90 and values of CMIN/df, RMSEA and SRMR are also within permissible limit, no items were further deleted to check improvements in the original model. The original scale is found to be fit for measuring emotional intelligence in the current sample.

4.5.1. Emotional Intelligence as a higher order construct

Empirical evidence shows that the four dimensions of emotional intelligence (self-emotion appraisal, others' emotion appraisal, use of emotion and regulation of emotion) make emotional intelligence a higher order construct (Wong & Law, 2002). To test how well the four dimensions represents emotional intelligence as a higher order construct, second order CFA was run on the data again using AMOS software.

Figure 4.4., represents the structure of emotional intelligence as a higher order construct consisting four first order constructs. As shown in figure paths were drawn from composite construct emotional intelligence to four dimensions of emotional intelligence. The whole structure represents emotional intelligence scale as a higher order reflective measure.

Figure 4.4. The second order CFA model of Emotional Intelligence Scale

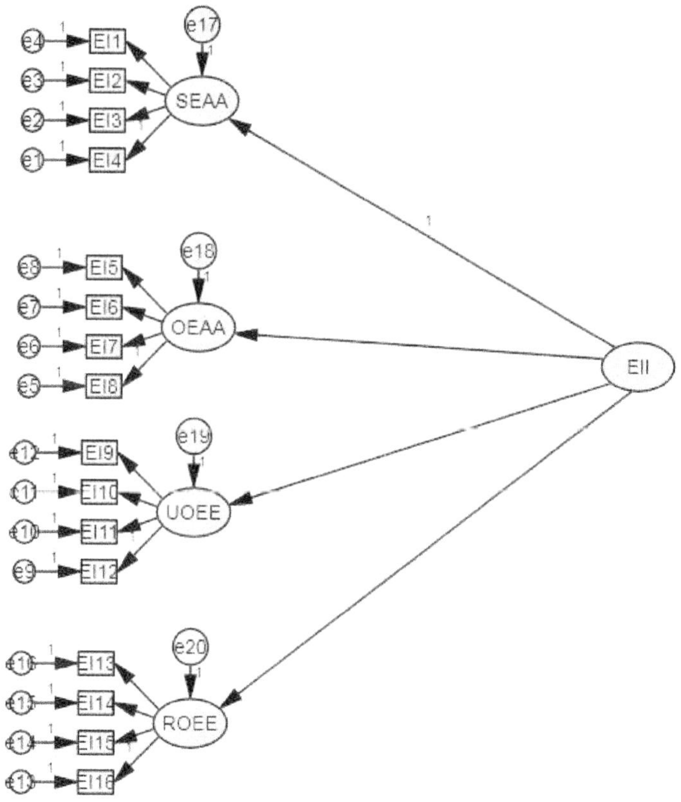

Table 4.5. Second order CFA Fit indices for Emotional Intelligence Scale

Model Fit Indices	Model 1 (original)
CMIN	181.581
df	100
p	<0.001
CMIN/df	1.816
GFI	.933
AGFI	.909
NFI	.938
TLI	.965
CFI	.971
RMSEA	.051
SRMR	0.0432

Table 4.5. shows the model fit indices of second order CFA of emotional intelligence scale. As we can see in the model, the value of GFI, AGFI, NFI, TLI, CFI, CMIN/df, RMSEA and SRMR are within their permissible range for good model fit and chi-square is also significant at 0.001 level, it can be concluded that the four dimensions; self-emotion appraisal, others' emotion appraisal, use of emotion and regulation of emotion reflect a larger theme of emotional intelligence. This model represents a hierarchical structure of emotional intelligence, in which the four dimensions compositely represent the higher construct of emotional intelligence.

Table 4.6., shows the factors, items and factor loadings of the final version of emotional intelligence scale in the current study.

Table 4.6. Factors, items and factor loadings of the final version of Emotional Intelligence Scale used in current study

Factor	Items	Factor loadings
Self-emotion appraisal	1. "I have a good sense of why I have certain feelings most of the time"	0.755
	2. "I have good understanding of my own emotions"	0.870
	3. "I really understand what I feel"	0.752
	4. "I always know whether or not I am happy"	0.725
Others' emotion appraisal	5. "I always know my friends' emotions from their behavior"	0.752
	6. "I am a good observer of others' emotions"	0.786
	7. "I am sensitive to the feelings and emotions of others"	0.694
	8. "I have good understanding of the emotions of people around me"	0.834
Use of emotion	9. "I always set goals for myself and then try my best to achieve them"	0.756
	10. "I always tell myself I am a competent person"	0.730
	11. "I am a self-motivating person"	0.877
	12. "I would always encourage myself to try my best"	0.869
Regulation of emotion	13. "I am able to control my temper so that I can handle difficulties rationally"	0.769

	14. "I am quite capable of controlling my own emotions"	0.846
	15. "I can always calm down quickly when I am very angry"	0.777
	16. "I have good control of my own emotions"	0.851

4.6. Big Five Inventory (John & Srivastava, 1999)

Confirmatory factor analysis was done on Big Five Inventory to test its proposed five-factor structure. The scale consists of 44 items, which measures five dimensions of individual's personality:

a) Extraversion - 8 items

b) Agreeableness-9 items

c) Conscientiousness- 9 items

d) Neuroticism- 8 items

e) Openness-10 items

First order confirmatory analysis was run to see factor loadings of the items and correlation among the five factors. Some widely accepted model fit indices including CMIN/df, GFI, AGFI, NFI, TLI, CFI, RMSEA and SRMR were also checked within their permissible limit to determine model fit. The recommended values for these fit indices guided the acceptability and fitness of the model (Hair et.al. 2018).

The first order confirmatory factor analysis of Big Five Inventory is shown in figure 4.5:

Figure 4.5. First order CFA of Big Five Inventory

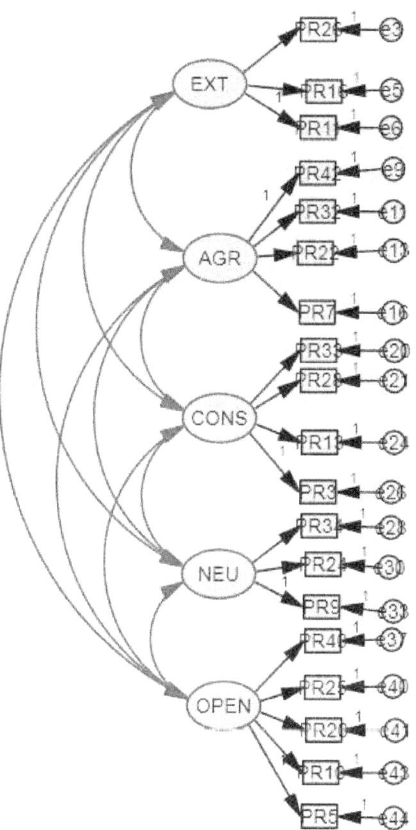

Table 4.7. Fit indices of the original Big Five Personality scale and the modified

version on current sample (First order CFA)

Model Fit Indices	Model 1	Model 2 Item 41 deleted	Model 3 Item 35 deleted	Model 4 Item 31 deleted	Model 5 Item 27 deleted	Model 6 Item 21 deleted
CMIN	2488.859	2383.528	2286.783	2142.702	2060.210	1916.622
df	892	851	810	770	731	693
CMIN/df	2.790	2.801	2.823	2.783	2.818	2.766
GFI	0.663	0.665	0.667	0.684	0.691	0.703
AGFI	0.626	0.627	0.629	0.647	0.653	0.666
NFI	0.515	0.520	0.530	0.546	0.556	0.573
TLI	0.595	0.600	0.608	0.625	0.632	0.651
CFI	0.618	0.623	0.631	0.648	0.655	0.674
RMSEA	0.076	0.076	0.077	0.076	0.077	0.075
SRMR	0.1027	0.1030	0.1036	0.1009	0.1010	0.0982
CHI SQUARE DIFFERENCE TEST		X^2 diff= 105.331 P< 0.01	X^2 diff= 96.745 P< 0.01	X^2 diff= 144.081 P< 0.01	X^2 diff= 82.492 P< 0.01	X^2 diff= 143.588 P< 0.01

Model Fit Indices	Model 7 Item 37 deleted	Model 8 Item 29 deleted	Model 9 Item 14 deleted	Model 10 Item 6 deleted	Model 11 Item 18 deleted	Model 12 Item 8 deleted
CMIN	1794.761	1664.195	1563.419	1440.252	1349.294	1231.030
df	656	620	585	551	518	486
CMIN/df	2.736	2.684	2.673	2.614	2.605	2.533
GFI	0.717	0.734	0.747	0.759	0.770	0.784
AGFI	0.680	0.698	0.712	0.724	0.736	0.751
NFI	0.588	0.605	0.619	0.637	0.649	0.669
TLI	0.666	0.684	0.697	0.715	0.726	0.746
CFI	0.688	0.706	0.718	0.736	0.747	0.766
RMSEA	0.075	0.074	0.073	0.072	0.072	0.070
SRMR	0.0965	.0924	0.0887	0.0861	0.0840	0.0813
CHI SQUARE DIFFERENCE TEST	X^2 diff= 121.861 P< 0.01	X^2 diff= 130.566 P< 0.01	X^2 diff= 100.776 P< 0.01	X^2 diff= 123.167 P< 0.01	X^2 diff= 90.958 P< 0.01	X^2 diff= 118.264 P< 0.01

Model Fit Indices	Model 13 Item 23 deleted	Model 14 Item 2 deleted	Model 15 Item 12 deleted	Model 16 Item 43 deleted	Model 17 Item 4 deleted	Model 18 Item 19 deleted
CMIN	1127.179	1021.167	934.732	857.033	797.761	731.065
df	455	425	396	368	341	315
CMIN/df	2.477	2.403	2.360	2.329	2.339	2.321
GFI	0.801	0.817	0.826	0.834	0.839	0.847
AGFI	0.769	0.786	0.796	0.804	0.809	0.817
NFI	0.686	0.705	0.721	0.736	0.747	0.760
TLI	0.763	0.783	0.797	0.810	0.817	0.828
CFI	0.783	0.801	0.815	0.827	0.835	0.846
RMSEA	0.069	0.067	0.066	0.65	0.066	0.065
SRMR	0.0779	0.0739	0.0716	0.0699	0.0688	0.0656
CHI SQUARE DIFFERENCE TEST	X^2 diff= 103.851 P< 0.01	X^2 diff= 106.01 P< 0.01	X^2 diff= 86.435 P< 0.01	X^2 diff= 77.699 P< 0.01	X^2 diff= 59.272 P< 0.01	X^2 diff= 66.696 P< 0.01

Model Fit Indices	Model 19 Item 39 deleted	Model 20 Item 1 deleted	Model 21 Item 38 deleted	Model 22 Item 15 deleted	Model 23 Item 36 deleted	Model 24 Item 17 deleted
CMIN	679.708	609.086	556.678	515.767	460.174	412.078
Df	290	266	243	221	200	180
CMIN/df	2.344	2.290	2.291	2.334	2.301	2.289
GFI	0.852	0.862	0.870	0.874	0.882	0.887
AGFI	0.821	0.832	0.840	0.843	0.851	0.856
NFI	0.771	0.787	0.797	0.804	0.816	0.827
TLI	0.835	0.849	0.875	0.858	0.868	0.875
CFI	0.853	0.866	0.873	0.876	0.885	0.893
RMSEA	0.066	0.065	0.065	0.066	0.065	0.064
SRMR	0.0648	0.0597	0.0592	0.0588	0.0573	0.0568
CHI SQUARE DIFFERENCE TEST	X^2 diff= 51.357 P< 0.01	X^2 diff= 70.622 P< 0.01	X^2 diff= 52.408 P< 0.01	X^2 diff= 40.911 P< 0.01	X^2 diff= 55.593 P< 0.01	X^2 diff= 48.096 P< 0.01

Model Fit Indices	Model 25 Item no.44 deleted	Model 26 Item no. 30 deleted
CMIN	371.496	293.835
df	160	142
CMIN/df	2.322	2.069
GFI	0.893	0.908
AGFI	0.860	0.877
NFI	0.837	0.862
TLI	0.880	0.907
CFI	0.899	0.923
RMSEA	0.065	0.059
SRMR	0.0534	0.0500
CHI SQUARE DIFFERENCE TEST	X^2 diff= 40.582 P< 0.01	X^2diff=77.661 P< 0.01

Table 4.7 shows the results of first order CFA of Big Five Personality scale. After conducting CFA on original scale, factor loadings of all the items and model fit indices were checked. Since, values of GFI, AGFI, NFI, TLI, CFI, RMSEA and SRMR are not within permissible limit for original scale, items were deleted consecutively as per their low values of factor loadings to get improvements in the model. Item no. 41, 35, 31, 27, 21, 37, 29, 14, 6, 18, 8, 23, 2, 12, 43, 4, 19, 39, 1, 38, 15, 36, 17, 44 and 30 (total 25 items) deleted one after another and improvements in model fit indices were checked for each model. Finally, CFA was concluded at model no. 26, as for this model values of CMIN/df, GFI, TLI, CFI, RMSEA and SRMR were within their permissible range. Hence model 26 is found to be best model for the inventory to be used for current sample.

The items deleted along with the factor they measure (in parenthesis), as per the order they were removed are listed below:

1. I see myself someone who has few artistic interests. (Openness)

2. I see myself someone who prefers work that is routine (Openness)

3. I see myself someone who is sometimes shy, inhibited. (Extraversion)

4. I see myself someone who can be cold and aloof. (Agreeableness)

5. I see myself someone who tends to be quiet.(Extraversion)

6. I see myself someone who is sometimes rude to others. (Agreeableness)

7. I see myself someone who can be moody.(Neuroticism)

8. I see myself someone who can be tense. (Neuroticism)

9. I see myself someone who is reserved. (Extraversion)

10. I see myself someone who tends to be disorganized. (Conscientiousness)

11. I see myself someone who can be somewhat careless (Conscientiousness)

12. I see myself someone who tends to be lazy. (Conscientiousness)

13. I see myself someone who tends to find fault with others. (Agreeableness)

14. I see myself someone who starts quarrels with others. (Agreeableness)

15. I see myself someone who is easily distracted. (Conscientiousness)

16. I see myself someone who is depressed, blue. (Neuroticism)

17. I see myself someone who worries a lot. (Neuroticism)

18. I see myself someone who gets nervous easily (Neuroticism)

19. I see myself someone who is talkative (Extraversion)

20. I see myself someone who makes plans and follows through with them

    (Conscientiousness)

21. I see myself someone who is ingenious, a deep thinker (Openness)

22. I see myself someone who is outgoing, sociable (Extraversion)

23. I see myself someone who has a forgiving nature. (Agreeableness)

24. I see myself someone who is sophisticated in art, music, or literature. (Openness)

25. I see myself someone who values artistic, aesthetic experiences.(Openness)

4.6.1. Personality as a higher order construct

Empirical evidence shows that there is no composite score for measuring individual's personality. Hence, the five dimensions of personality do not make personality as a higher order construct (Goldberg, 1993).

The final version of the scale used in current study with factors, items and factor loadings is shown in Table 4.8.

Table 4.8. Factors, items and factor loadings of the final version of Big Five Inventory used in current study

Factor	Items	Factor loadings
Extraversion	1. "I see myself someone who is full of energy"	0.736
	2. "I see myself someone who generates a lot of enthusiasm"	0.678
	3. "I see myself someone who has an assertive personality"	0.573
Agreeableness	4. "I see myself someone who is helpful and unselfish with others"	0.584

	5. "I see myself someone who is generally trusting"	0.674
	6. "I see myself someone who is considerate and kind to almost everyone"	0.680
	7. "I see myself someone who likes to cooperate with others"	0.682
Conscientiousness	8. "I see myself someone who does a thorough job "	0.545
	9. "I see myself someone who is a reliable worker "	0.695
	10. "I see myself someone who perseveres until the task is finished"	0.607
	11. "I see myself someone who does things efficiently"	0.713
Neuroticism	12. "I see myself someone who is relaxed, handles stress well "	0.672
	13. "I see myself someone who is emotionally stable, not easily upset"	0.739
	14. "I see myself someone who remains calm in tense situations"	0.648
Openness	15. " I see myself someone who is original, comes up with new ideas"	0.707
	16. " I see myself someone who is curious about many different things"	0.593
	17. " I see myself someone who has an active imagination"	0.538
	18. " I see myself someone who is inventive"	0.637

	19. " I see myself someone who likes to reflect, play with ideas"	0.572

4.7. Mental Health Inventory-38 (Veit & Ware, 1983)

To assess mental health of managers the Mental Health Inventory-38 (Veit & Ware, 1983) has been used. The inventory consists of 38 items, which can be aggregated into six subscales (Anxiety, Depression, Loss of Behavioral/Emotional Control, General positive effect, Emotional ties and Life satisfaction), or two global scales (Psychological Distress and Psychological Well-being) and a global Mental Health Index score.

In the preset study confirmatory factor analysis has been done to test the two factor structure (Psychological distress & Psychological well-being) and a composite mental health factor of the inventory.

4.7.1 First order confirmatory analysis of two factor structure of mental health

First order confirmatory analysis was done to test its proposed two-factor structure. The scale consists of 38 items, which measures two dimensions of mental health:

a) Psychological Distress- 24 items

b) Psychological Well-being- 14 items

CFA was run to see factor loadings of the items and correlation among the two dimensions. Some widely accepted model fit indices including GFI, AGFI, NFI, TLI, CFI, RMSEA and SRMR were also checked within their permissible limit to determine model fit. The recommended values for these fit indices guided the acceptability and fitness of the model (Hair et.al. 2018).

The first order confirmatory factor analysis of mental health inventory is shown in figure below.

4.6. First order CFA of Mental Health Inventory

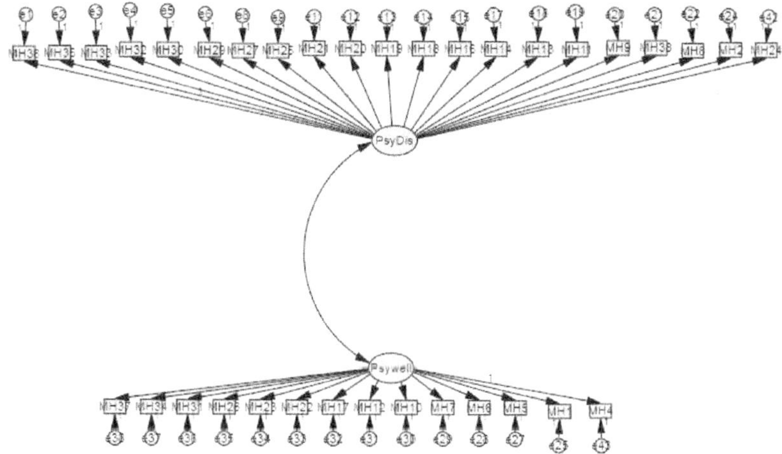

Table 4.9. Fit indices of the original Mental Health Inventory and the modified version on current sample (First order CFA)

Model Fit Indices	Model 1	Model 2 Item no. 28 removed	Model 3 Item no.3 removed	Model 4 Item no. 15 removed	Model 5 Item no. 4 removed
CMIN	1426.874	1332.552	1280.806	1198.331	1162.791
Df	664	628	593	559	526
CMIN/df	2.149	2.122	2.160	2.144	2.211
GFI	0.788	0.797	0.799	0.808	0.809
AGFI	0.764	0.773	0.774	0.784	0.784
NFI	0.798	0.808	0.813	0.821	0.823
TLI	0.873	0.881	0.822	0.889	0.887
CFI	0.880	0.888	0.889	0.895	0.894
RMSEA	0.061	0.060	0.061	0.061	0.062
SRMR	0.0644	0.0625	0.0626	0.0595	0.0598
CHI SQUARE DIFFERENCE TEST		X^2diff=94.322 P<0.01	X^2diff=51.746 P<0.05	X^2diff=82.475 P<0.01	X^2diff=35.54 P>0.05

Table 4.9 shows results of first order CFA of mental health inventory. It includes the fit indices of original mental health inventory and the modified version of the inventory on the current sample. After conducting CFA on original mental health inventory, factor loadings of the all items were checked. Among all items, item no. 28 had lowest factor loading, so the item 28 was removed to get better model fit. After removing item 28, there was an improvement in model fit indices in the model 2, but not up to the required range. Hence, factor loadings of items were further checked and it was found that item no.3 had lowest factor loading among all. So, item no.3 was removed to see improvement in model 3. There was an improvement in model fit indices in model 3, but again not up to the required range. Further factor loadings of items were checked and it was found that item no.15 had lowest factor loading. After deleting item no. 15, there was a significant

improvement in model 4. The values of TLI (0.889), CFI (0.895), RMSEA (0.061) and SRMR (0.0595) were almost in their permissible limit. Further, another model (Model 5) was tested after deleting item no.4 to check better model fit, but there was no improvement in the model 5 and chi-square difference test was also found to be insignificant. Hence, CFA was concluded at Model 4 and it was accepted as best model for the inventory.

The items deleted along with the factor they measure (in parenthesis), as per the order they were removed are listed below:

1. During the past month, did you think about taking your own life? (Psychological Distress)

2. How often did you become nervous or jumpy when faced with excitement or unexpected situations during the past month? (Psychological Distress)

3. During the past month, how often did your hands shake when you tried to do something? (Psychological Distress)

4.7.2. Mental health as a higher order construct

Authors have conceptualized mental health as a higher-order construct, but it was concluded that reliance on a single mental health score can be associated with significant loss of information (Veit & Ware, 1983).

To test higher order structure of mental health, second order CFA was conducted on the current sample. During CFA, the higher order structure was not showing significant model fit, rather the variance of higher order mental health construct was found to be negative (-0.638). Hence, it was concluded that the two factors; Psychological distress and Psychological well-being do not make mental health as a composite construct on current sample.

The final version of inventory along with factors, items and factor loadings is shown in Table 4.10.

Table 4.10 Factors, items and factor loadings of the final version of Mental Health Inventory used in current study

Factor	Items	Factor loadings
Psychological Distress	1. "How much of the time have you felt lonely during the past month?"	0.594
	2. "During the past month, have you had any reason to wonder if you were losing your mind, or losing control over the way you act, talk, think, feel, or of your memory?"	0.581
	3. "Did you feel depressed during the past month?"	0.592
	4. "How much of the time, during the past month, have you been a very nervous person?"	0.607
	5. "During the past month, how much of the time have you felt tense or high-strung?"	0.761
	6. "During the past month, have you been in firm control of your behaviour, thoughts, emotions or feelings?"	0.559
	7. "During the past month, how often	0.616

	did you feel that you had nothing to look forward to?"	
	8. "How much of the time, during the past month, have you felt emotionally stable?"	0.705
	9. "How much of the time, during the past month, have you felt downhearted and blue?"	0.822
	10. "How often have you felt like crying, during the past month?"	0.770
	11. "During the past month, how often have you felt that others would be better off if you were dead?"	0.615
	12. "How often, during the past month, did you feel that nothing turned out for you the way you wanted it to?"	0.530
	13. "How much have you been bothered by nervousness, or your nerves, during the past month?"	0.671
	14. "How often, during the past month, have you felt so down in the dumps that nothing could cheer you up?"	0.707
	15. "During the past month, how much of the time have you felt restless, fidgety, or impatient?"	0.770
	16. "During the past month, how much of the time have you been moody or brooded about things?"	0.689

	17. "During the past month, how often did you get rattled, upset or flustered?"	0.707
	18. "During the past month, have you been anxious or worried?"	0.762
	19. "How often during the past month did you find yourself trying to calm down?	0.571
	20. "During the past month, how much of the time have you been in low or very low spirits?"	0.845
	21. "During the past month, have you been under or felt you were under any strain, stress or pressure?"	0.723
Psychological Well-being	22. "How happy, satisfied or pleased have you been with your personal life during the past month?"	0.697
	23. "During the past month, how much of the time have you felt that the future looks hopeful and promising?"	0.527
	24. "How much of the time, during the past month, has your daily life been full of things that were interesting to you?"	0.696
	25. "How much of the time, during the past month, did you feel relaxed and free from tension?"	0.690
	26. "During the past month, how much of the time have you generally enjoyed the things you	0.734

	do?”	
	27. “During the past month, how much of the time have you felt loved and wanted?”	0.601
	28. “When you have got up in the morning, this past month, about how often did you expect to have an interesting day?”	0.593
	29. “How much of the time, during the past month, have you felt calm and peaceful?”	0.753
	30. “How much of the time, during the past month, were you able to relax without difficulty?”	0.682
	31. “How much of the time, during the past month, did you feel that your love relationships, loving and being loved were full and complete?”	0.692
	32. “During the past month, how much of the time has living been a wonderful adventure for you?”	0.562
	33. “How much of the time, during the past month, have you felt cheerful, light hearted?”	0.768
	34. “During the past month, how much of the time were you a happy person?”	0.802
	35. “How often, during the past month, have you been waking up feeling fresh and rested?”	0.660

This chapter describes the analyses and results of quantitative as well as qualitative part of the study. The chapter is divided into two sections; Section I and Section II. Under the section I, analysis and results of quantitative study are explained and under the section II analysis and results of qualitative study are explained.

Section I : Quantitative Data Analysis and Results

It includes descriptive analysis of demographic variables, t-test and correlation analysis between studied variables, moderation analysis and simple slope analysis. Results are reported in the form of tables and figures with brief description and interpretation of the findings. On the basis of the results hypotheses were checked for their acceptance or rejection.

5.1. Descriptive analysis

5.1.1. Demographic characteristics of the sample

To study the characteristics of sample, mean, standard deviation, frequency and percentage of demographic variables like age, educational qualification, type of organization, total work experience, marital status, duration of marriage, number of children, number of dependent elders, distance of workplace from the residence and income per month of participants were analyzed.

Table 5.1 Mean and SD of demographic variables (N=311)

Demographic variables	Mean	SD
Age (Years)	34.08	8.60
Total work experience (years)	10.57	8.40
Duration of marriage (years)	7.89	8.84

From Table 5.1, it can be inferred that the average age of the participants was 34.08 (SD=8.6) years. The average work experience was 10.57 (SD=8.40) years and average duration of marriage was 7.89 (SD=8.84) years.

Table 5.2 Frequency and Percentage of demographic variables (N=311)

Demographic variables	Frequency	Percentage
Type of Organization		
Government	158	50.80%
Private	153	49.19%
Educational Qualification		
Graduate	133	42.76%
Post-graduate	167	53.69%
Other	11	3.53%
Marital Status		
Single	98	31.51%
Married	210	67.52%
Other(Widow/Divorced/Engaged)	03	0.96%
Number of children		
Zero	144	46.30%
One	77	24.75%
Two	84	27.00%
Three	5	1.60%
Four or more	1	0.32%
Number of dependent elders		
Zero	216	69.45%

One	35	11.25%
Two or more	60	19.30%
Type of family		
Nuclear	194	62.37%
Joint	82	26.36%
Living independently	35	11.25%
Distance of workplace from residence (km)	-	-
1-5 km	74	23.79%
5-10 km	55	17.68%
10-15 km	74	23.79%
Above 15 km	108	34.72%
Income per month (Rs.)	-	-
10,000-30,000	66	21.22%
30,000-50,000	82	26.36%
50,000-70,000	65	20.90%
Above 70,000	98	31.51%

From Table 5.2, it can be inferred that almost equal number of managers from government and private sector organizations participated in the study. Majority of the participants were post-graduate. Some of them have additional qualifications like Diploma, Executive courses etc. Most of the participants were married, living in nuclear families with monthly income more than Rs.70, 000.

5.1.2. Testing for Normality

There are various statistical tests to check the normality of the data. Skewness and kurtosis are one of the important statistical characteristics which used to describe the normality of distribution (Hair, Black, Babin & Anderson, 2018). Skewness is the measure of symmetry of the distribution, while kurtosis is the measure of whether the data are heavy-tailed or light-tailed relative to normal distribution. According to George and Mallery (2010), the values of skewness and kurtosis between -2 and +2 are considered acceptable in order to prove normal distribution.

Analysis of skewness and kurtosis values for current sample showed that the values are within the range of +/- 2, The skewness values ranged from -0.020 (Work-life balance 7) to -1.806 (Personality 13) and the kurtosis value ranged from 0.008 (Mental health 33) to 1.862 (Mental health 21). Therefore it can be concluded that the current data is little skewed and kurtotic, but does not differ significantly from normality. Hence, parametric tests can be applied to analyze the data to check formulated hypotheses.

Table 5.3. Descriptive statistics (Mean, SD, Skewness & Kurtosis) of questionnaire items

Construct	Items	Mean	SD	Skewness	Kurtosis
Work-life balance (WLB)	WLB1	4.20	1.42	0.143	0.055
	WLB2	4.71	1.47	-0.151	-0.334
	WLB3	4.42	1.57	0.034	-0.597
	WLB4	4.43	1.53	-0.055	-0.549
	WLB5	4.09	1.45	0.158	-0.154
	WLB6	4.57	1.54	-0.136	-0.573
	WLB7	3.78	1.73	-0.020	-0.876
	WLB8	4.94	1.57	-0.344	-0.394
	WLB9	5.39	1.44	-0.587	-0.141

	WLB10	5.90	1.26	-0.961	0.226
	WLB11	5.96	1.30	-1.296	1.429
	WLB12	3.31	1.82	0.583	-0.604
	WLB13	3.68	1.72	0.317	-0.656
	WLB14	3.30	1.74	0.575	-0.532
	WLB15	3.56	1.73	0.400	-0.676
Emotional Intelligence (EI)	EI1	5.37	1.55	-1.102	0.678
	EI2	5.78	1.45	-1.374	1.394
	EI3	5.63	1.62	0.138	0.834
	EI4	5.87	1.39	-1.420	1.659
	EI5	5.50	1.33	-1.049	1.082
	EI6	5.46	1.42	-0.919	0.383
	EI7	5.86	1.27	-1.302	1.600
	EI8	5.61	1.29	-0.977	0.774
	EI9	5.75	1.45	-1.238	0.966
	EI10	5.69	1.41	-1.215	1.153
	EI11	5.87	1.42	-1.295	1.058
	EI12	6.09	1.27	-1.629	2.301
	EI13	5.37	1.55	-0.796	-0.285
	EI14	5.22	1.62	-0.777	-0.266

	EI15	4.87	1.80	-0.625	-0.620
	EI16	5.19	1.73	-0.857	-0.181
Personality (PR)	PR3	4.19	0.90	-1.112	1.135
	PR5	3.90	0.94	-0.776	0.390
	PR7	4.30	0.93	-1.571	1.589
	PR9	2.37	1.06	0.567	-0.348
	PR10	4.05	0.97	-0.975	0.461
	PR11	4.01	0.98	-0.922	0.362
	PR13	4.50	0.78	-1.806	1.463
	PR16	3.96	0.91	-0.600	-0.204
	PR20	3.97	0.93	-0.981	0.959
	PR22	4.40	0.90	-1.797	1.306
	PR24	2.45	1.14	0.398	-0.743
	PR25	3.68	0.96	-0.505	0.037
	PR26	3.82	0.95	-0.487	-0.277
	PR28	4.08	0.91	-0.844	0.385
	PR32	4.25	0.85	-1.386	1.485
	PR33	4.29	0.84	-1.292	1.784
	PR34	2.23	1.01	0.659	-0.214
	PR40	3.72	0.94	-0.429	-0.252

	PR42	4.34	0.80	-1.566	1.335
Mental Health (MH)	MH1	3.99	1.07	-0.345	-0.140
	MH2	2.55	1.30	0.608	-0.401
	MH4	4.22	1.20	-0.677	-0.237
	MH5	3.69	1.26	-0.273	0.779
	MH6	3.44	1.27	-0.041	-0.763
	MH7	4.01	1.21	-0.395	-0.631
	MH8	2.59	1.38	0.716	-0.200
	MH9	2.11	1.16	1.279	1.032
	MH10	4.18	1.22	-0.461	-0.388
	MH11	2.24	1.12	0.860	0.452
	MH12	3.97	1.31	-0.040	-0.815
	MH13	2.92	1.14	0.261	-0.304
	MH14	2.63	1.06	0.341	-0.071
	MH16	2.38	1.29	0.777	0.016
	MH17	4.00	1.20	-0.390	-0.585
	MH18	2.82	1.44	0.356	-0.915
	MH19	2.47	1.25	0.750	0.015
	MH20	2.61	1.24	0.387	-0.481
	MH21	1.82	1.25	1.597	1.862

	MH22	3.79	1.36	-0.181	-0.912
	MH23	4.07	1.47	-0.587	-0.616
	MH24	3.11	1.33	0.384	-0.503
	MH25	2.26	1.27	0.893	-0.061
	MH26	3.42	1.38	-0.065	-0.952
	MH27	2.60	1.40	0.560	-0.674
	MH29	2.50	1.23	0.735	-0.065
	MH30	2.69	1.15	0.529	-0.131
	MH31	3.99	1.14	-0.354	-0.768
	MH32	2.72	1.09	0.610	0.815
	MH33	2.60	1.17	0.720	0.008
	MH34	4.12	1.17	-0.635	-0.349
	MH35	3.13	1.18	0.390	-0.016
	MH36	2.52	1.29	0.739	-0.117
	MH37	3.84	1.11	-0.037	-0.267
	MH38	2.95	1.39	0.349	-0.804

5.1.3 t-test analysis

In the present research 158 women managers from government and 153 women managers from private sector organizations participated in the study. To see the difference on the dimensions of work-life balance, mental health, emotional intelligence and personality between women managers working in government and private sector organizations, t-test analysis was performed. The results are reported in Table 5.2.3.

Table 5.4. Mean, SD, t-value and p-value of Women managers working in Government and Private organizations on the dimensions of Work-life balance, Mental health, Emotional Intelligence and Personality.

Dimensions	WM-Government organizations (n=158)		WM-Private organizations (n=153)		t-value	p-value	Cohen's d
	Mean	SD	Mean	SD			
WIPL	30.02	7.99	30.41	8.30	0.42	0.67	0.04
PLIW	22.31	4.38	22.05	4.36	0.52	0.60	0.06
WPLE	13.30	5.44	14.43	6.06	1.73	0.08	0.19
WLB	65.63	10.65	66.90	12.20	0.97	0.32	0.10
PsyD	52.13	18.20	56.41	18.07	2.07	**0.03***	**0.23**
PsyW	55.13	12.72	54.31	11.79	0.58	0.557	0.06
SEA	23.21	4.63	22.08	5.36	1.99	**0.04***	**0.22**
OEA	23.00	4.27	22.25	6.81	1.17	0.24	0.13
UOE	23.69	4.43	23.10	5.13	1.07	0.28	0.12
ROE	20.91	5.60	20.37	5.98	0.82	0.41	0.09
EI	90.80	14.44	87.80	17.74	1.64	0.10	0.18
EXT	11.91	2.27	11.76	2.22	0.57	0.56	0.06
AGR	17.75	2.43	16.82	2.77	3.16	**0.002***	**0.35**

CONS	17.50	2.55	16.59	2.54	3.12	**0.002***	**0.35**
NEUR	7.01	2.54	7.09	2.66	0.28	0.77	0.03
OPEN	19.06	3.44	19.49	3.29	1.11	0.26	0.12
d(effect size)=0.2 (small); *d*=0.5(medium); *d*=0.8(large)							

Note: N=311, WM: Women Managers; WIPL: Work Interference with Personal Life; PLIW: Personal Life Interference with Work; WPLE: Work/Personal Life Enhancement; WLB: Work-Life Balance; PsyD: Psychological Distress; PsyW: Psychological Wellbeing; SEA: Self Emotion Appraisal; OEA: Others' Emotion Appraisal; UOE: Use of Emotion; ROE: Regulation of Emotion; EI: Emotional Intelligence; EXT: Extraversion; AGR: Agreeableness; CONS: Conscientiousness; NEUR: Neuroticism; OPEN: Openness

As shown in Table 5.4, there is no significant difference between women managers working in government sector organizations and women managers working in private sector organizations on the dimensions of work-life balance (work interference with personal life, personal life interference with work & work/personal life enhancement). However, the two groups differ significantly on the dimensions of psychological distress, self emotion appraisal, agreeableness and consciousness with small effect size. By observing the mean scores we can conclude that, women managers working in private sector organizations (Mean= 56.41) experience more psychological distress as compared to managers working in government sector organizations (Mean= 52.13). In context of emotional intelligence and personality, women managers working in government sector organizations score high on self emotion appraisal, agreeableness and consciousness as compared to women managers working in private sector organizations.

Thus, the hypothesis *H1* which states that there would be a significant difference between women managers working in government sector organizations and women managers working in private sector organizations on the dimension of work-life balance (work interference with personal life, personal life interference with work, work-personal life enhancement), mental health (psychological distress and psychological wellbeing), emotional intelligence (self-emotion appraisal, others' emotion appraisal, use of emotions, regulation of emotion) and personality (extraversion, openness, agreeableness, conscientiousness and neuroticism) is partially accepted.

5.2. Correlation analysis

To study the relationship between variables under the study i.e. work-life balance, mental health, emotional intelligence and personality of women managers, correlation analysis was performed. The results are shown in Table 5.5.

Table 5.5. Correlations among dimensions of study variables

Variables	1	2	3	4	5	6	7	8	9	10	11	12	13	14	15	16
1.WIPL	1															
2.PLIW	.39**	1														
3.WPLE	.26**	.18**	1													
4.WLB	.85**	.65**	.62**	1												
5.PsyD	-.37**	-.36**	-.38**	-.51**	1											
6.PsyW	.48**	.38**	.41**	.59**	-.72**	1										
7.SEA	.17**	.26**	.25**	.30**	-.38**	.29**	1									
8.OEA	.05	.11*	.16**	.13*	-.24**	.18**	.41**	1								
9.UOE	.07	.20**	.31**	.24**	-.34**	.30**	.53**	.39**	1							
10. ROE	.24**	.15**	.23**	.29**	-.32**	.32**	.45**	.40**	.44**	1						
11.EI	.18**	.24**	.31**	.32**	-.42**	.36**	.77**	.74**	.75**	.77**	1					
12.EXT	.11*	.20**	.28**	.25**	-.31**	.36**	.33**	.31**	.50**	.37**	.55**	1				
13.AGR	.07	.19**	.18**	.19**	-.31**	.16**	.38**	.34**	.43**	.41**	.51**	.53**	1			
14.CONS	.04	.25**	.24**	.21**	-.34**	.25**	.39**	.33**	.51**	.37**	.52**	.59**	.67**	1		
15.NEUR	-.18*	-.19**	-.20**	-.26**	-.44**	-.44**	-.40**	-.21**	-.35**	-.57**	-.51**	-.45**	-.37**	-.40**	1	
16.OPEN	.08	.16**	.23**	.20**	-.26**	.28**	.34**	.33**	.51**	.35**	.50**	.63**	.52**	.53**	-.49**	1

Effect size (Cohen,1992) : r=0.1 (small); 0.3(medium); 0.5 (large)

Note: N=311, WIPL: Work Interference with Personal Life; PLIW: Personal Life Interference with Work; WPLE: Work/Personal Life Enhancement; WLB: Work-Life Balance; PsyD: Psychological Distress; PsyW: Psychological Wellbeing; SEA: Self Emotion Appraisal; OEA: Others' Emotion Appraisal; UOE: Use of Emotion; ROE: Regulation of Emotion; EI: Emotional Intelligence; EXT: Extraversion; AGR: Agreeableness; CONS: Consciousness; NEUR: Neuroticism; OPEN: Openness

*$p < 0.05$, **$p < 0.01$

As shown in Table 5.5 there is a significant positive correlation between work-life balance and psychological well-being, while there is a significant negative correlation between work-life balance and psychological distress. Emotional intelligence has been found to be significantly and positively related with work-life balance and psychological well-being, while negatively related with psychological distress. Apart from this, all four dimensions of personality; extraversion, consciousness, agreeableness and openness have been found to be positively related with psychological well-being and emotional intelligence and negatively related with psychological distress, while neuroticism has been found to be significantly and negatively related with work-life balance, psychological well-being and emotional intelligence, while positively related with psychological distress.

Hence, the second hypothesis *H2,* which states that there is a significant relationship between dimensions of work-life balance, mental health, emotional intelligence and personality, has been partially accepted.

5.3. Moderation analysis

To see the moderating effect of emotional intelligence and personality, moderation analysis was done on software PROCESS macro (version 2.16) for SPSS, developed by Andrew F. Hayes (2017).

5.3.1. Emotional intelligence as moderator

Table 5.6 shows the moderating effect of emotional intelligence on the relationship between work-life balance and psychological distress.

Table 5.6. Moderation analysis of emotional intelligence on work-life balance and psychological distress

Model summary							
R	R^2	MSE	F	df1	df2	P	
0.51	0.26	249.76	35.29	3.00	307.00	<.001	
Model							
	b value	SE	T	LLCI	ULCI	p-value	
Constant	66.29	24.50	2.71	18.07	114.51	0.01	
EI	0.16	0.27	0.61	-0.37	0.69	0.54	
WLB	0.45	0.37	1.19	-0.29	1.18	0.23	
WLB x EI(int_1)	-0.01	0.00	-2.31	-0.02	0.00	**0.02***	

N=311; ΔR^2 (int_1) = 0.01, p*<0.05

As shown in Table 5.6. The interaction between work-life balance and emotional intelligence (WLB x EI) on psychological distress is found to be significant (p=0.02), which indicates that there is a moderating effect of emotional intelligence on the relationship of work-life balance and psychological distress of women managers.

Figure 5.1 Graphical representation of interaction between work-life balance and emotional intelligence on psychological distress

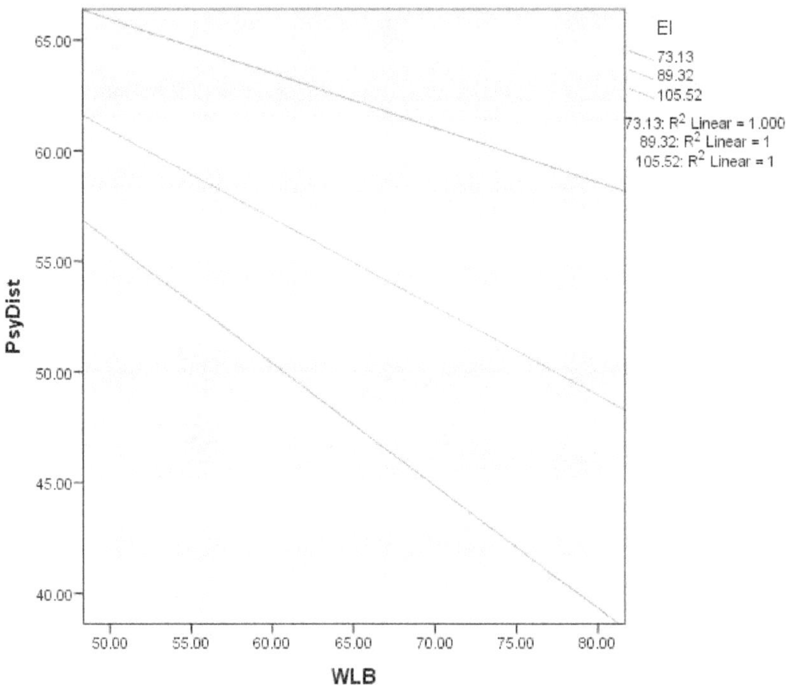

To further confirm the moderating effect of emotional intelligence we conducted simple slope analysis (Fig 5.1). As shown in Figure, work-life balance (WLB) is negatively related with psychological distress (PsyDist) at all three level of emotional intelligence (EI), but effect of work-life balance on psychological distress is greatest for managers having high emotional intelligence (b=-0.55, p< 0.001), followed by managers having average emotional intelligence (b=-0.40, p< 0.001), and least for managers having low emotional intelligence (b=-0.25, p=0.02). Hence the level of emotional intelligence influences the relationship of work-life balance and psychological distress of women managers. Thus, our third hypothesis *H3*, which states that there would be a moderating role of emotional intelligence on the relationship of work-life balance and psychological distress of women managers, is accepted.

Table 5.7 shows the moderating effect of emotional intelligence on the relationship between work-life balance and psychological well-being.

Table 5.7. Moderation analysis of emotional intelligence on work-life balance and psychological well-being

Model summary						
R	**R^2**	**MSE**	**F**	**df1**	**df2**	**P**
0.49	0.24	115.47	32.22	3.00	307.00	<.001
Model						
	b-value	**SE**	**T**	**LLCI**	**ULCI**	**p-value**
Constant	36.39	16.66	2.18	3.61	69.18	0.03
EI	-0.05	0.18	-0.27	-0.41	0.31	0.79
WLB	-0.07	0.25	-0.27	-0.57	0.43	0.78
WLB x EI(int_2)	0.00	0.00	1.65	0.00	0.01	0.10

N=311; ΔR^2 (int_2) = 0.01, p*<0.05

As shown in Table 5.7 the interaction between work-life balance and emotional intelligence (WLB x EI) on psychological well-being is not significant (p=0.10), which indicates that there is no moderating effect of emotional intelligence on the relationship of work-life balance and psychological well-being of women managers. Thus our fourth hypothesis *H4*, which states that there would be a moderating role of emotional intelligence on the relationship of work-life balance and psychological wellbeing of women managers, is rejected.

5.3.2. Personality as moderator

Since, the five dimensions (extraversion, agreeableness, conscientiousness, openness, and neuroticism) of personality do not make personality as a composite construct, we analyzed moderating role of each dimension separately on the relationship of work-life balance and mental health (psychological distress and psychological well-being) of women managers.

A) Extraversion as moderator

The trait extraversion describes someone who is assertive, enthusiastic, active, energetic, outgoing and talkative (McCrae & John, 1992). The moderating role of extraversion has been examined first on the relationship of work-life balance and psychological distress and again on the relationship of work-life balance and psychological well-being of women managers.

Table 5.8 shows the moderating effect of extraversion on the relationship between work-life balance and psychological distress.

Table 5.8. Moderation analysis of Extraversion on Work-life balance and Psychological Distress

Model summary						
R	R^2	MSE	F	df1	df2	P
0.44	0.19	270.41	24.78	3.00	307.00	<.001
Model						
	b-value	SE	T	LLCI	ULCI	p-value
Constant	21.11.	30.27	0.70	-38.46	80.67	0.49
EXT	5.04	2.46	2.05	0.20	9.89	0.04
WLB	0.92	0.45	2.03	0.03	1.81	0.04
WLB x EXT (int_3)	-0.11	0.04	-3.04	-0.18	-0.04	**<0.001***

N=311; ΔR^2 (int_3) = 0.02, p*<0.01

As shown in Table 5.8. The interaction between work-life balance and extraversion (WLB x EXT) on psychological distress is found to be significant (p<0.001), which indicates that there is a moderating effect of extraversion on the relationship of work-life balance and psychological distress of women managers.

Figure 5.2.Graphical representation of interaction between work-life balance and extraversion on psychological distress.

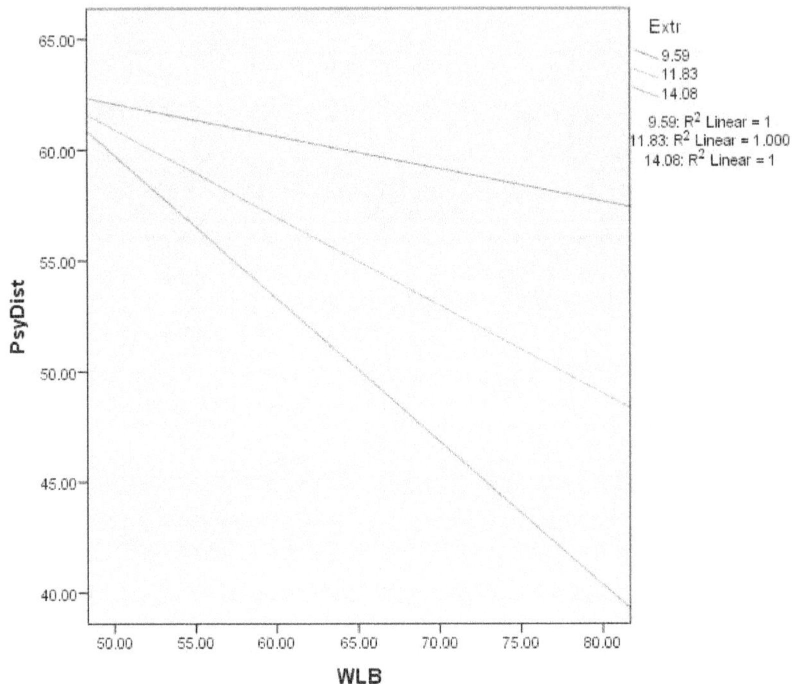

To further confirm the moderating effect of extraversion we conducted simple slope analysis (Fig .5.2.) As shown in Figure, work-life balance (WLB) is negatively related with psychological distress (PsyDist) at all three level of extraversion (Extr), but effect of work-life balance on psychological distress is greatest for managers having high extraversion (b=-0.65, p< 0.001), followed by managers having average extraversion (b=-0.40, p< 0.001), and least for managers having low extraversion (b=-0.15, p=0.24).

Hence, the level of extraversion shows a moderating effect on the relationship of work-life balance and psychological distress of women managers.

Table 5.9 shows the moderating effect of extraversion on the relationship between work-life balance and psychological well-being of women managers.

Table 5.9. Moderation analysis of Extraversion on Work-life balance and Psychological Well-being

Model summary						
R	**R^2**	**MSE**	**F**	**df1**	**df2**	**P**
0.50	0.25	113.61	34.42	3.00	307.00	<.001
Model						
	b-value	**SE**	**T**	**LLCI**	**ULCI**	**p-value**
Constant	49.13	19.62	2.50	10.52	87.74	0.01
EXT	-1.41	1.60	-0.88	-4.55	1.73	0.38
WLB	-0.25	0.29	-0.84	-0.82	0.33	0.40
WLB x EXT (int_4)	0.05	0.02	2.07	0.00	0.10	**0.04***

N=311; ΔR^2 (int_2) = 0.01, p*<0.05

As shown in Table 5.9. The interaction between work-life balance and extraversion (WLB x Extr) on psychological well-being is found to be significant (p= 0.04), which indicates that there is a moderating effect of extraversion on the relationship of work-life balance and psychological well-being of women managers.

Figure 5.3. Graphical representation of interaction between work-life balance and extraversion on psychological well-being

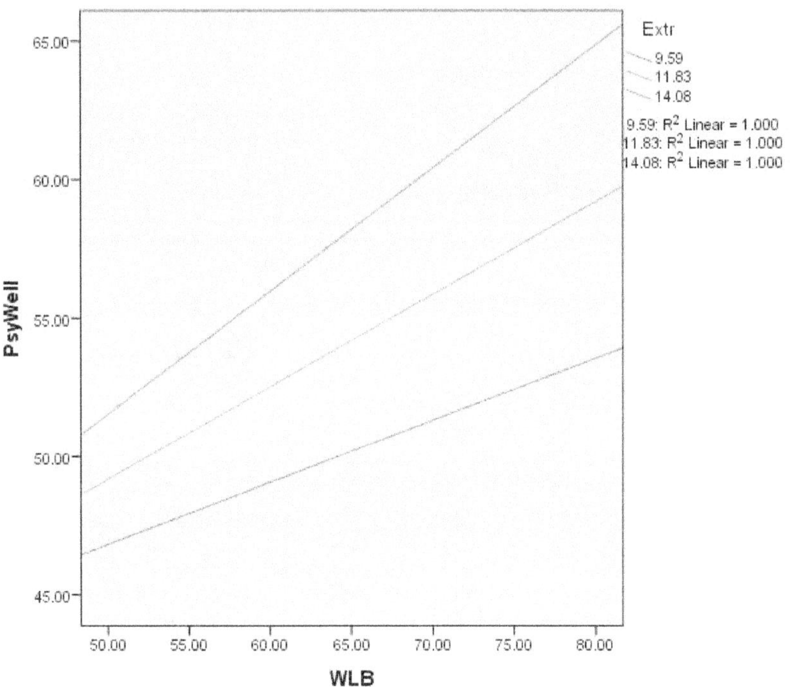

To further confirm the moderating effect of extraversion, we conducted simple slope analysis (Fig. 5.3). As shown in Figure, work-life balance (WLB) is positively related with psychological well-being (PsyWell) at all three level of extraversion (Extr), but effect of work-life balance on psychological well-being is greatest for managers having high extraversion (b= 0.44, p< 0.001), followed by managers having average extraversion (b= 0.33, p< 0.001), and least for managers having low extraversion (b= 0.22, p=0.01).

Hence the level of extraversion shows moderating effect on the relationship of work-life balance and psychological well-being of women managers.

B) Agreeableness as moderator

The trait agreeableness describes someone who is cooperative, sympathetic, altruistic, compliant, kind, forgiving and trusting (McCrae & John, 1992). The moderating role of agreeableness has been examined first on the relationship of work-life balance and psychological distress and again on the relationship of work-life balance and psychological well-being of women managers.

Table 5.10 shows the moderating effect of agreeableness on the relationship between work-life balance and psychological distress.

Table 5.10. Moderation analysis of Agreeableness on Work-life balance and Psychological Distress

Model summary						
R	R^2	MSE	F	df1	df2	P
0.44	0.19	271.74	24.16	3.00	307.00	<.001
Model						
	b-value	SE	T	LLCI	ULCI	p-value
Constant	31.91.	35.56	0.90	-38.06	101.88	0.37
AGR	3.04	2.05	1.48	-0.99	7.07	0.14
WLB	0.89	0.54	1.65	-0.17	1.94	0.10
WLB x AGR(int_5)	-0.08	0.03	-2.51	-0.14	-0.02	**0.01***

N=311; ΔR^2 (int_5) = 0.02, p*<0.05

As shown in Table 5.10. The interaction between work-life balance and agreeableness (WLB x AGR) on psychological distress is found to be significant (p=0.01), which indicates that there is a moderating effect of agreeableness on the relationship of work-life balance and psychological distress of women managers.

Figure 5.4. Graphical representation of interaction between work-life balance and Agreeableness on psychological distress

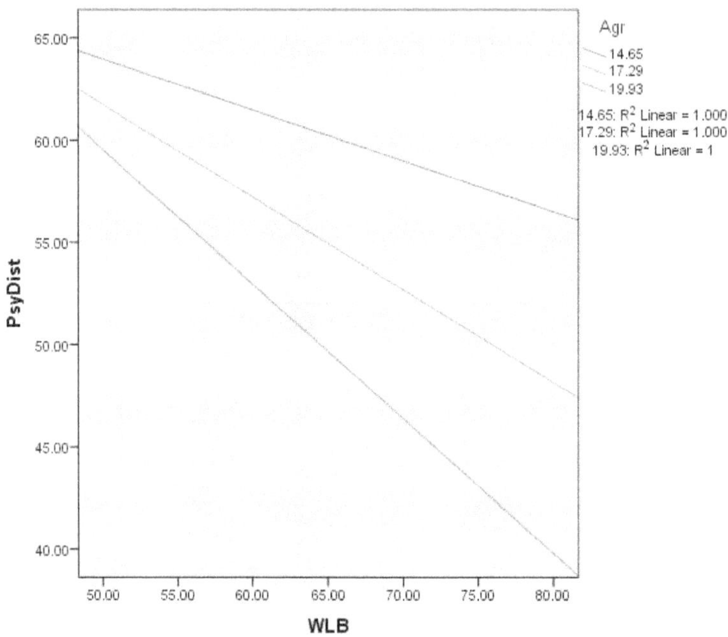

To further confirm the moderating effect of extraversion we conducted simple slope analysis. As shown in Figure 5.4, work-life balance (WLB) is negatively related with psychological distress (PsyDist) at all three level of agreeableness (AGR), but effect of work-life balance on psychological distress is greatest for managers having high agreeableness (b=-0.66, p< 0.001), followed by managers having average agreeableness (b=-0.45, p< 0.001), and least for managers having low agreeableness (b=-0.25, p=0.03). Hence, the level of agreeableness shows a moderating effect on the relationship of work-life balance and psychological distress of women managers.

Table 5.11 shows the moderating effect of agreeableness on the relationship between work-life balance and psychological well-being of women managers.

Table 5.11. Moderation analysis of Agreeableness on Work-life balance and Psychological Well-being

Model summary						
R	**R^2**	**MSE**	**F**	**df1**	**df2**	**P**
0.41	0.16	126.88	20.12	3.00	307.00	<.001
Model						
	b-value	**SE**	**T**	**LLCI**	**ULCI**	**p-value**
Constant	78.69	24.30	3.24	30.88	126.50	<0.001
AGR	-2.84	1.40	-2.03	-5.59	-0.09	0.04
WLB	-0.55	0.37	-1.49	-1.27	0.18	0.14
WLB x AGR(int_6)	0.05	0.02	2.53	0.01	0.09	**0.01***

N=311; ΔR^2 (int_6) = 0.02, p*<0.05

As shown in Table 5.11 the interaction between work-life balance and agreeableness (WLB x AGR) on psychological well-being is found to be significant (p=0.01), which indicates that there is a moderating effect of agreeableness on the relationship of work-life balance and psychological well-being of women managers.

Figure 5.5. Graphical representation of interaction between work-life balance and agreeableness on psychological well-being

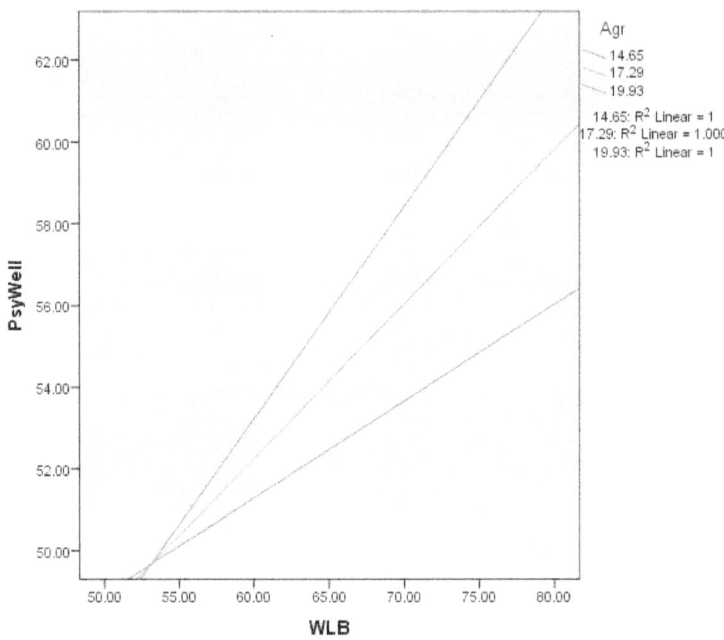

To further confirm the moderating effect of agreeableness, we conducted simple slope analysis (Fig 5.5) As shown in Figure, work-life balance (WLB) is positively related with psychological well-being (PsyWell) at all three level of agreeableness (AGR), but effect of work-life balance on psychological well-being is greatest for managers having high agreeableness (b=0.52, p< 0.001), followed by managers having average agreeableness (b=0.38, p< 0.001), and least for managers having low agreeableness (b=0.24, p<0.001). Hence the level of agreeableness shows moderating effect on the relationship of work-life balance and psychological well-being of women managers.

C) Conscientiousness as moderator

The trait conscientiousness describes someone who is achievement oriented, hard working, efficient, organized, dependable, responsible, and systematic (Judge & Higgins, 1999; McCrae & John, 1992). The moderating role of conscientiousness has been examined first on the relationship of work-life balance and psychological distress and again on the relationship of work-life balance and psychological well-being of women managers.

Table 5.12 shows the moderating effect of conscientiousness on the relationship between work-life balance and psychological distress.

Table 5.12. Moderation analysis of Conscientiousness on Work-life balance and Psychological Distress

Model summary						
R	R^2	MSE	F	df1	df2	P
0.46	0.22	263.67	28.03	3.00	307.00	<.001
Model						
	b-value	SE	T	LLCI	ULCI	p-value
Constant	34.90.	35.46	0.98	-34.87	104.68	0.33
Cons	2.78	2.02	1.38	-1.19	6.75	0.17

| WLB | 0.90 | 0.53 | 1.70 | -0.14 | 1.95 | 0.09 |
| WLB x Cons(int_7) | -0.08 | 0.03 | -2.58 | -0.14 | -0.02 | **0.01*** |

N=311; ΔR^2 (int_7) = 0.02, p*<0.05

As shown in Table 5.12 the interaction between work-life balance and conscientiousness (WLB x Cons.) on psychological distress is found to be significant (p=0.01), which indicates that there is a moderating effect of conscientiousness on the relationship of work-life balance and psychological distress of women managers.

Figure 5.6. Graphical representation of interaction between work-life balance and conscientiousness on psychological distress

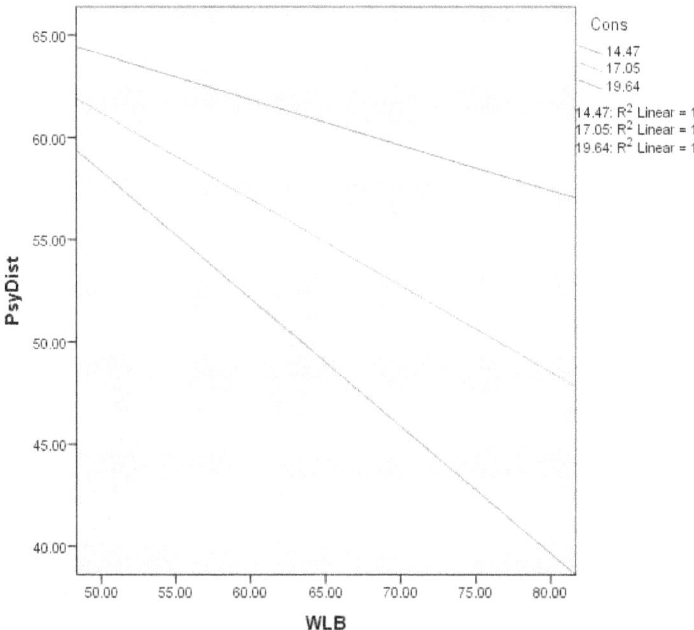

To further confirm the moderating effect of conscientiousness we conducted simple slope analysis (Fig. 5.6). As shown in Figure, work-life balance (WLB) is negatively related with psychological distress (PsyDist) at all three level of conscientiousness (Cons.), but effect of work-life balance on psychological distress is greatest for managers having high conscientiousness (b=-0.62, p<0.001), followed by managers having average conscientiousness (b=-0.42, p<0.001), and least for managers having low conscientiousness (b=-0.22, p=0.07). Hence, the level of conscientiousness shows a moderating effect on the relationship of work-life balance and psychological distress of women managers.

Table 5.13 shows the moderating effect of conscientiousness on the relationship between work-life balance and psychological well-being of women managers.

Table 5.13. Moderation analysis of Conscientiousness on Work-life balance and Psychological Well-being

Model summary						
R	**R²**	**MSE**	**F**	**df1**	**df2**	**P**
0.44	0.20	121.86	25.16	3.00	307.00	<.001
Model						
	b-value	**SE**	**T**	**LLCI**	**ULCI**	**p-value**
Constant	65.22.	24.11	2.71	17.79	112.66	0.01
Cons	-1.99	1.37	-1.45	-4.69	0.70	0.15
WLB	-0.45	0.36	-1.26	-1.16	0.26	0.21
WLB x Cons(int_8)	0.05	0.02	2.31	0.01	0.09	**0.02***

N=311; ΔR^2 (int_8) = 0.01, p*<0.05

As shown in Table 5.13 the interaction between work-life balance and consciousness (WLB x Cons) on psychological well-being is found to be significant (p=0.02), which indicates that there is a moderating effect of consciousness on the relationship of work-life balance and psychological well-being of women managers.

Figure 5.7. Graphical representation of interaction between work-life balance and conscientiousness on psychological well-being

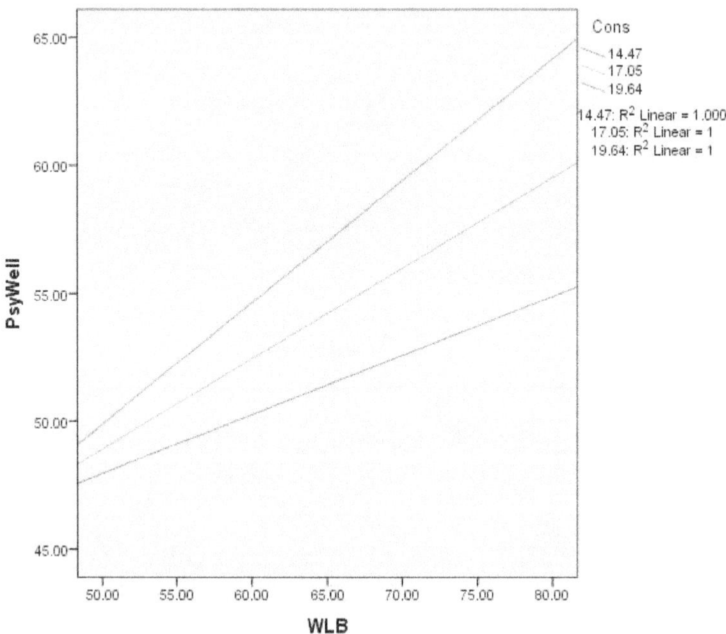

To further confirm the moderating effect of conscientiousness, we conducted simple slope analysis (Fig. 5.7). As shown in Figure, work-life balance (WLB) is positively related with psychological well-being (PsyWell) at all three level of conscientiousness (Cons.), but effect of work-life balance on psychological well-being is greatest for managers having high conscientiousness (b= 0.48, p< 0.001), followed by managers having average conscientiousness (b= 0.35, p<0.001), and least for managers having low conscientiousness (b= 0.23, p< 0.001). Hence the level of conscientiousness shows moderating effect on the relationship of work-life balance and psychological well-being of women managers.

D) Openness as moderator

The trait openness is characterized by intelligence, creativity, curiosity, unconventionality, imagination and originality (Barrick & Mount,1991; McCrae & John,1992). The moderating role of openness has been examined first on the relationship of work-life balance and psychological distress and again on the relationship of work-life balance and psychological well-being of women managers.

Table 5.14 shows the moderating effect of openness on the relationship between work-life balance and psychological distress.

Table 5.14 Moderation analysis of Openness on Work-life balance and Psychological Distress

Model summary						
R	**R^2**	**MSE**	**F**	**df1**	**df2**	**P**
0.40	0.16	281.88	19.61	3.00	307.00	<.001
Model						
	b-value	**SE**	**T**	**LLCI**	**ULCI**	**p-value**
Constant	50.28.	32.17	1.56	-13.02	113.59	0.12
Open	1.67	1.60	1.05	-1.47	4.82	0.30
WLB	0.45	0.48	0.95	-0.49	1.39	0.35
WLB x Open(int_9)	-0.05	0.02	-1.92	-0.09	0.00	0.06

N=311; ΔR^2 (int_9) = 0.01, p*<0.05

As shown in Table 5.14 the interaction between work-life balance and openness (WLB x Open) on psychological distress is not significant (p=0.06), which indicates that there is no moderating effect of openness on the relationship of work-life balance and psychological distress of women managers.

Table 5.15 shows the moderating effect of openness on the relationship between work-life balance and psychological well-being of women managers.

Table 5.15. Moderation analysis of Openness on Work-life balance and Psychological well-being

Model summary						
R	**R^2**	**MSE**	**F**	**df1**	**df2**	**P**
0.45	0.21	120.68	26.41	3.00	307.00	<.001
Model						
	b-value	**SE**	**T**	**LLCI**	**ULCI**	**p-value**
Constant	47.66.	21.05	2.26	6.24	89.08	0.02
Open	-0.84	1.05	-0.81	-2.90	1.22	0.42
WLB	-0.17	0.31	-0.55	-0.79	0.44	0.58
WLB x Open (int_10)	0.03	0.02	1.76	0.00	0.06	0.08

N=311; ΔR^2 (int_9) = 0.01, p*<0.05

As shown in Table 5.15 the interaction between work-life balance and openness (WLB x Open) on psychological well-being is not significant (p=0.08), which indicates that there is no moderating effect of openness on the relationship of work-life balance and psychological well-being of women managers.

E) Neuroticism as moderator

The trait neuroticism refers to anxiety, worry, tension, insecurity and defensiveness (Judge & Higgins; McCrae & John, 1992). The moderating role of neuroticism has been examined first on the relationship of work-life balance and psychological distress and again on the relationship of work-life balance and psychological well-being of women managers.

Table 5.16 shows the moderating effect of neuroticism on the relationship between work-life balance and psychological distress.

Table 5.16 Moderation analysis of Neuroticism on Work-life balance and Psychological Distress

Model summary						
R	**R^2**	**MSE**	**F**	**df1**	**df2**	**P**
0.51	0.26	248.92	35.75	3.00	307.00	<.001
Model						
	b-value	**SE**	**T**	**LLCI**	**ULCI**	**p-value**
Constant	76.85.	14.47	5.31	48.39	105.32	<0.001
NEUR	0.26	2.03	0.13	-3.74	4.27	0.90
WLB	-0.65	0.21	-3.03	-1.07	-0.23	<0.001
WLB x NEUR (int_11)	0.04	0.03	1.31	-0.02	0.10	0.19

N=311; ΔR^2 (int_11) = 0.00, p*<0.05

As shown in Table 5.16 the interaction between work-life balance and neuroticism (WLB x NEUR) on psychological distress is not significant (p=0.19), which indicates that there is no moderating effect of neuroticism on the relationship of work-life balance and psychological distress of women managers.

Table 5.17 shows the moderating effect of neuroticism on the relationship between work-life balance and psychological well-being of women managers.

Table 5.17. Moderation analysis of Neuroticism on Work-life balance and Psychological well-being

Model summary						
R	R^2	MSE	F	df1	df2	P
0.54	0.30	106.84	43.09	3.00	307.00	<.001
Model						
	b-value	SE	T	LLCI	ULCI	p-value
Constant	31.67.	9.48	3.34	13.02	50.32	<0.001
NEUR	0.37	1.33	0.28	-2.25	2.99	0.78
WLB	0.55	0.14	3.94	0.28	0.83	<0.001
WLB x NEUR (int_12)	-0.04	0.02	-1.74	-0.07	0.00	0.08

N=311; ΔR^2 (int_11) = 0.01, p*<0.05

As shown in Table 5.17 the interaction between work-life balance and neuroticism (WLB x NEUR) on psychological well-being is not significant (p=0.08), which indicates that there is no moderating effect of neuroticism on the relationship of work-life balance and psychological well-being of women managers.

Since, some of the dimensions (extraversion, agreeableness & conscientiousness) show moderating effect on the relationship of work-life balance and psychological distress as well as on the relationship of work-life balance and psychological well-being but other dimensions (openness & neuroticism) do not, the hypotheses *H5* and *H6* are partially accepted.

Section II : Qualitative Data Analysis and Results

Qualitative study was conducted to gain deeper insight of participant's perception about work-life balance and mental health issues, which were not measurable from quantitative data alone. To know the views of participants, semi-structured interviews were conducted on 6 participants.

Inclusion Criteria: i) Women manager

ii) Married

iii) Having at least one pre-school going child.

The inclusion criteria were set on the basis of evidence from past literature. According to Roehling, Roehling and Moen's (2001), conflict between work and family life increases as one's responsibility towards family expands through marriage and the arrival of children . Degree of work-family conflict is related to parental responsibility. Parents with children of 5 years or younger (pre-school) experience highest degree of conflict, followed by parents with school aged children (above 5 years) and least conflict for parents having no children. The degree of conflict decreases as the age of youngest child increases (Roehling, Roehling & Moen, 2001; Higgings et. al. 1994). By setting the inclusion criteria we maintained a reasonable amount of homogeneity in the sample.

Following research questions were asked to tap the views of participants:

a) How do you perceive your work-life balance?

b) What is the impact of your work-life balance on your mental health?

c) What strategies you follow to achieve a good work-life balance and mental health?

d) What is the role of your family in achieving a good work-life balance?

e) What is the role of your organization in achieving a good work-life balance?

Data were analyzed through **Interpretive Phenomenological Analysis (IPA)**. IPA is influenced by theoretical tradition of phenomenology and hermeneutics. Phenomenology is the "study of human experience and the way in which things are perceived as they appear to consciousness" (Langdridge, 2007). Hermeneutics was initially devised to interpret the Biblical texts but now widely known as "Theory of interpretation" (Shaw, 2010). The central objective of IPA is to understand the meaning of personal and social experiences of people, which they encounter or feel. It is an empathetic method in which researcher tries to understand the experiences of respondent's from their perspective. The results are drawn in the form of clusters, themes and sub-themes and interpreted in a logical manner.

The results of present qualitative study in the form of clusters, themes and sub-themes with supportive extracts are shown in Table 5.18.

Table 5.18. Results of IPA of semi-structured interviews

Cluster	Themes	Sub-themes	Supporting extract
1. Meaning of Work-life balance	A. Individual perception	a. Work and family needs.	*" If I fulfill my duties at home as well as at my workplace, I consider my work and personal life are balanced"*
		b. Happiness	*"For me work-life balance is being happy with my work and my personal life."*
	B. Individual experience	a. Conflict	*"My parents have health issues, sometimes I have to leave them because of work"*
		b. Facilitation	*"My wok gives me opportunity to learn "*
		c. Personal journey	*"Work and family go hand-in-hand. If I would not have been working, my life would be a miserable life"*
2. Social Support	A. Role of family	a. Spouse support	*"Spouse is very-very important in achieving your work-life balance, because he is the mediator between you and the in-laws and setting the expectations right."*
			"I live in nuclear family. My spouse is very supportive, that's why I am working."
		b. In-laws support	*"When I come to office, my mother-in-law takes care of my one and half year old son."*

	B. Role of Other's	a. Domestic help	*"I don't take extra load from work as well as from home side. Cook comes and cooks the food for the family."*
		b. Childcare support	*"The school has crèche facility. After school, my daughter stays in crèche while I am in office."*
3. Organizational Culture	A. Organizational support	a. Formal support	*"The organization provides family friendly policies like maternity leaves, childcare leaves and child education allowance etc."*
		b. Informal support	*"If there is any emergency at home, we just call or message our senior. There is an understanding in the culture."*
	B. Informal group	a. Role of colleagues	*"More than formal policies, it is your understanding with colleagues, which makes your life easier".*
		b. Effective Communication	*"If I plan any leave, I inform my senior as well as my juniors before hand, they manage, and work doesn't suffer in my absence"*
4. Work-life balance and	A. Impact of conflict on mental	a. Stress	*"When there is six days working in office, home works remain pending; it creates stress in my mind."*

Mental health	health	b. Burnout	*"Sometimes I feel so much overloaded that I tell my boss, that I will not be able to handle that much work".*
	B. Impact of balance on mental health	a. Sense of achievement	*"I get pleasure, feeling proud of my work."*
		b. Self- identity	*"Kaam kar ke achha lagta hai, I have my own identity, I can take decisions myself."*
		c. Contentment	*"I enjoy my work and I am very much satisfied with my life."*
	C. Strategies for achieving good work-life balance	a. Prioritizing	*"I prioritize office and personal works as per their importance and urgency"*
		b. Time management	*"After finishing my work at office, I rush for home. I never waste my time in office gossips."*
	D. Strategies for good mental health	a. Exercise	*"I do regular exercise to stay physically and mentally fit."*
		b. Meditation	*"To get the peace of mind I have started meditation."*
		c. Recreational activities	*"I need outings in every two or three months, otherwise I feel irritated and exhausted".*
		d. Open communication	*"If I feel stressed I vent out my feelings to my family members."*

Through the analysis of qualitative data **4 clusters** (Meaning of work-life balance, Social support, Organizational culture & Work-life balance and mental health), **10 themes** and **24 sub-themes** have emerged, which will be discussed in the next chapter under discussion.

The present research studied the work-life balance, mental health, emotional intelligence and personality of women managers working in different sector of organization. Quantitative analysis, which included descriptive analysis, correlation, group comparison and moderation analysis, was conducted to explore the relationship of work-life balance and mental health of women managers and to examine the moderating role of emotional intelligence and personality on this relationship. In addition, qualitative analysis which included Interpretive Phenomenological Analysis (IPA), was done to assess and document the underlying perception and views of women managers (n=8) regarding their work-life balance and mental health issues.

In the present chapter, results and findings of quantitative and qualitative analysis will be discussed in detail. The chapter is divided into two sections; Section I and Section II. Under the section I, results and findings of quantitative analysis will be discussed and under the section II results and findings of qualitative data analysis will be discussed.

6.1. Section I : Quantitative Data Inference

In the quantitative part of a study total 311 women managers were participants, in which 158 women managers were from government sector organizations and 153 women managers from private sector organizations of Delhi and NCR. Majority of the participants were post-graduate. Some had additional qualification like Diploma and executive degrees as well. Most of the participants were married (67.52%) living in nuclear (62.37%) family. 46.30% of participants had no children, while rest of the participants was having one, two, three, four or more children. Some of participants

(30.55%) had responsibility of dependent elders as well. The average age of the participants was 34.08 years while average work experience was 10.57 years.

Data was analyzed to test six formulated hypotheses for the study. The findings of the study in the light of formulated hypotheses and existing literature is discussed under following headings:

6.1.1. Difference between women managers from government organizations and women from private organizations on the dimension of work-life balance (work interference with personal life, personal life interference with work & work/personal life enhancement), mental health (psychological distress & psychological wellbeing), emotional intelligence (self-emotion appraisal, others' emotion appraisal, use of emotions, regulation of emotion) and personality (extraversion, openness, agreeableness, conscientiousness and neuroticism)

To see the difference between women managers from government sector organizations and women managers from private sector organizations on the dimensions of work-life balance, mental health, emotional intelligence and personality hypothesis *HI* was formulated and data was analyzed through t-test. From the result of t-test (Table 5.4), it was found that there is no significant difference between women managers from government sector organizations and women managers from private sector organizations on the dimensions of work-life balance (work interference with personal life, personal life interference with work & work/personal life enhancement). However, the two groups differ significantly on the dimensions of psychological distress, self emotion appraisal, agreeableness and conscientiousness. It has been also found that women managers working in private sector organizations (Mean= 56.41) experience more psychological distress in comparison to women managers working in government sector organizations (Mean= 52.13). In context of emotional intelligence and personality, women managers working in government sector organizations scored high on self emotion appraisal, agreeableness and conscientiousness when compared to women managers working in private sector organizations. To understand these differences, the findings are discussed under the light of existing literature. According to Gayathri and Karthikeyan (2013), economic liberalization and availability of skilled cheap workers have made India an attractive destination for multinational corporations. Due to the job opportunities available in abundance the women participation in workforce has also increased. The entries of women employees and changing nature of work have made both government and private sector organizations to consider work-life balance issues strategically. The companies are now realizing that they need to adopt strategic human resource practices similar to western countries. Both government and private sector organizations are providing maternity leave, paternity leave, part-time work, work-from home, and flexible working hours to support work-life balance of their employees. For government organizations, offering work-life balance programs is more like complying with government regulations and labor laws, while for private organization it is used as a strategic tool to retain talented employees. This could be the reason; the two groups in the present study did not show significant difference on the dimensions of work-life balance.

It has been also found that the women managers working in private sector organizations experience more psychological distress than women managers working in government sector organizations. This difference is because the implementation of work-life balance programs is more effective in government sector organizations in comparison to private sector organization (Baral & Bhargava, 2011; Buelens & Broeck, 2007). The government sector organizations provide more supportive environment to their employees. There are reduced work hours in government organizations in comparison to private sector organization. The employees of government sector organizations get more time for private life and longer resting hours, which has a positive effect on their mental health (Buelens & Broeck, 2007).

Being mentally healthy, employees of government organizations also able to conserve their personal resources more efficiently than employees of private sector organizations, hence score high on dimensions of emotional intelligence (self emotion appraisal) and personality (agreeableness and conscientiousness).

6.1.2. Relationship between study variables (Work-life balance, Mental health, Emotional intelligence & personality)

To see the relationship between dimensions of work-life balance, mental health, emotional intelligence and personality, hypothesis *H2* was formulated. Data was analyzed through product-moment correlation analysis. Results (Table 5.5) indicated that, there is a significant positive correlation between work-life balance and psychological well-being, while there is a significant negative correlation between work-life balance and psychological distress of women managers. The findings are in the line of existing literature. Work-life balance has been found to be predictor of employee's well-being (Vallone & Donaldson, 2001). Conflict between work and family leads to psychological depression (Googins,1991). Haar, Russo, Sune and Ollier-Malaterre (2014) in their study on 1416 employees from seven different culture- Malaysian, Spanish, French, New Zealand European, New Zealand Maori, Chinese, and Italian, found that work-life balance was positively related to job and life satisfaction, while negatively related to anxiety and depression in all seven populations. Frone (2000) examined the relationship between work-family balance and several types of psychiatric disorders like mood, anxiety, substance dependence and substance abuse on the representative national sample of 2700 employed adults, who were either married or the parent of child 18 years old or younger. Data was analyzed through hierarchical logistic regression analysis, which revealed that individuals who experience work-to-family conflict were more likely to have mood disorder, anxiety disorder and substance dependence disorder than individuals experiencing no work-to-family conflict.

From Table 5.5 it has been also found that emotional intelligence is significantly and positively related with work-life balance and psychological well-being, while negatively related with psychological distress. Apart from this, all four dimensions of personality; extraversion, consciousness, agreeableness and openness have been found positively related with psychological well-being and emotional intelligence and negatively related with psychological distress, while neuroticism has been found to be significantly and negatively related with work-life balance, psychological well-being and emotional intelligence, while positively related with psychological distress. Empirical evidence shows that emotional intelligence contributes positively in various life domains including work, family and relationships (Goleman, 1995; Salovey & Mayer, 1990). Since, emotional intelligence is the ability to understand and regulate one's own as well as other's emotions, it helps in building healthy relationships (Schutte et.al. 2001).

Furthermore, it has been also found that emotional intelligence is associated with less depression, higher emotional-wellbeing, higher optimism and self-esteem (Schutte et,al. 2001; Schutte et, al. 2002). Gupta and Kumar (2010) in their study on 200 college students of Kurukshetra University, India found that emotional intelligence is positively correlated with self-efficacy and mental health of the participants. They also reported that male participants scored high on self-efficacy and mental health in comparison to female participants. Hence, the relationship is more crucial for female participants. They recommended training and intervention programs for women in India to improve their emotional intelligence, which will eventually have a positive impact on their self-efficacy and mental health.

In context of personality, results are in the line of existing literature. Research shows personality as a strong predictor of happiness. It has been found that extraversion is positively related while neuroticism is negatively related to happiness (Furnham & Christoforou, 2007). Chamorro-Premuzic, Bennett and Furnham (2007) found that extraversion, conscientiousness, agreeableness and stability were positively correlated with happiness and emotional intelligence which explained 18% of unique variance in happiness. In addition, Weiss et al. (2008) found that extraversion, agreeableness, conscientiousness and openness are positively correlated, while neuroticism is negatively correlated with subjective well-being (happiness). They argued that personality and happiness share a common genetic structure. Happiness is accounted by unique genetic factor which influences from neuroticism, extraversion and conscientiousness and by a common genetic factor that influences all five factors of personality in the direction of low neuroticism and high extraversion, openness, agreeableness and conscientiousness.

6.1.3. Emotional Intelligence (EI) as moderator

6.1.3.1. Moderating role of emotional intelligence on the relationship between work-life balance and psychological distress

To examine the moderating role of emotional intelligence on the relationship of work-life balance and psychological distress, hypothesis *H3* was formulated. Data was analyzed through moderation analysis using software PROCESS macro (version 2.16) for SPSS. From the analysis it was found that, the interaction between work-life balance and emotional intelligence (WLB x EI) on psychological distress was significant (p=0.02), which indicated that there is a moderating effect of emotional intelligence on the relationship of work-life balance and psychological distress of women managers (Table 5.6). In addition, results of simple slope analysis (Figure 5.1) revealed that the level of emotional intelligence influences the effect of work-life balance on the mental health of women managers. Work-life balance has been found to be negatively related with psychological distress at all three level (High, average & low) of emotional intelligence, but effect of work-life balance on psychological distress was greatest for managers having high emotional intelligence (b=-0.55, p< 0.001), followed by managers having average emotional intelligence (b=-0.40, p< 0.001), and least for managers having low emotional intelligence (b=-0.25, p=0.02). These findings can be interpreted in the light of conservation of resource theory and existing literature. From the perspective of conservation of resource theory, emotional intelligence has emerged as personal resource, which has a potential to minimize the psychological distress experienced by the women managers while juggling with work and personal life. Similar kind of results has been found by other researchers in context of work-life balance and work/individual outcomes.

For example, Lenaghan, Buda and Eisner (2007) in their study on 205 employees found that emotional intelligence plays a moderating role on the relationship of work-family conflict and well-being of employees. It minimizes the negative impact of work-family conflict on the well-being of employees. Results showed that, employees having higher emotional intelligence with low work-family conflict reported higher well-being in comparison to employees having low emotional intelligence and high work-family conflict. Emotional intelligence has been found to be negatively related with depression (Carton et al.1999), anxiety (Bastian et al. 2005), feeling of worry and distress while dealing with a challenging task (Matthews et.al. 2006). Goleman (1995) stated that "keeping our distressing emotion in check is the key to emotional well-being". He argued that emotional intelligence has the potential to check those distressing emotions and contribute significantly in positive life outcomes. Gao et al. (2012) in his study on 212 high school teachers in China, has found that emotional intelligence plays a moderating role on the relationship of work-family conflict and job satisfaction of the employees. It weakens the impact of work-family conflict on job satisfaction of the employees. Carmeli (2003) explored the moderating role of emotional intelligence on work-family conflict and career commitment of 98 senior managers in Israel. Results revealed that, emotional intelligence plays a moderating role on the relationship of work-family conflict and career commitment of senior managers. Work-family conflict was negatively related to career commitment of managers, but the effect was low for managers having high emotional intelligence in comparison to managers having low emotional intelligence. Hence, the existing literature supports the results obtained in the present study.

6.1.3.2. Moderating role of emotional intelligence on the relationship between work-life balance and psychological well-being.

To examine the moderating role of emotional intelligence on the relationship of work-life balance and psychological well-being, hypothesis *H4* was formulated. Again, data was analyzed through moderation analysis using software PROCESS macro (version 2.16) for SPSS. From the analysis it was found that, the interaction between work-life balance and emotional intelligence (WLB x EI) on psychological well-being was not significant (p=0.10), which indicated that there is no moderating effect of emotional intelligence on the relationship of work-life balance and psychological well-being of women managers (Table 5.7). The result slightly deviates from the existing literature. Literature shows that, emotional intelligence plays a moderating role on the relationship of, work-family conflict and well-being (Lenaghan, Buda & Eisner, 2007), work-family conflict and job satisfaction (Gao et.al. 2012) and, role conflict and job stress (Dasgupta & Mukherjee, 2011). However, some of the research studies also support the obtained result. For example, Carmeli (2003) explored the moderating role of emotional intelligence on the relationship of work-family conflict and job satisfaction. Study was conducted on 98 senior managers employed as chief financial officers in government organizations of Israel. Data was analyzed through hierarchical regression analysis. Results showed that the interaction between emotional intelligence and work-family conflict on job satisfaction was not significant, which indicated that emotional intelligence had no moderating effect on the relationship of work-family conflict and job satisfaction of senior managers.

Slaski (2001) studied the role of emotional intelligence on quality of work-life, morale, distress, general mental health and managerial performance of middle and senior managers from UK. Data was collected from 224 middle and senior managers on the measures of study variables. Results of the study indicated that emotional intelligence was moderately related to morale (r= 0.55), quality of work-life (r=0.41), distress (r= -0.57), and general mental health (r= -0.50). Furthermore, management performance was found to be very modestly related with the dimensions of emotional intelligence. It was found to be modestly correlated with intrapersonal factor of EI (r=0.23), but negligibly with the inter-personal factor (r=0.01) and weakly with stress management (r=0.15) and adaptability (r=0.18). In addition, an intervention study was conducted simultaneously with this sample, in which two groups were formed; an experimental group and a control group. The emotional intelligence training program was conducted on the experimental group for six months, to see the effect of emotional intelligence on the managerial performance of managers. After six months, the performance of experimental group was compared with the control group (statistically controlling the initial EQ scores), it was found that there was no significant improvements in the performance of experimental group in comparison to the control group. Critically evaluating the concept of EI, Barrett et. al (2001) argued that the role of EI in personal and occupational success is exaggerated and impressionistically stated in the theory and literature.

In the present research we have found the similar results. From the results it has been found that emotional intelligence has a positive relationship with work-life balance and psychological well-being separately (Table 5.5), but the moderation effect of EI on the relationship between work-life balance and psychological well-being is not significant (Table 5.7).

From the above discussions, it can be concluded that emotional intelligence act as personal resource in balancing work and family life, but the role of EI is more significant on the relationship of work-life balance and psychological distress in comparison to work-life balance and psychological well-being. Thus it is indicating that we may not need to use our emotional intelligence when things are customary or when the well-being is good, we only use our emotional intelligence when the situation is stressful or when we are in distress.

6.1.4. Dimensions of Personality as moderators

6.1.4.1. Extraversion: The trait extraversion describes someone who is assertive, enthusiastic, active, energetic, outgoing and talkative (McCrae & John, 1992). In the present research, moderating role of extraversion was examined on the relationship of work-life balance and psychological distress and, work-life balance and psychological well-being of women managers. From Table 5.8 it has been found that the interaction between work-life balance and extraversion (WLB x Extr) on psychological distress is significant (p< 0.001), which confirmed the moderating role of extraversion on the relationship of work-life balance and psychological distress of women managers. Similarly, from Table 5.9 it has been found that the interaction between work-life balance and extraversion (WLB x Extr) on psychological well-being is also significant (p=0.04), which indicated that extraversion has a moderating effect on the relationship of work-life balance and psychological well-being of women managers. The findings are in the line of existing literature. According to Wayne, Nicholas and Fleeson (2002), two characteristics of extraverts i.e. positivity and high energy make them capable to handle conflict and embrace facilitation. Due to high energy levels, extraverts are likely to handle more tasks in less time without experiencing more fatigue in comparison to introverts. They also like to feel less strain and pressure in handling demanding tasks. By focusing on positive aspects of situation, they perceive the situation less stressful. In context of facilitation, extraverts more likely to experience positive affect (Diener & Lucas, 1999), readily attend to positive events, and more strongly react to them (Rusting & Larsen, 1998).

Ghorpade, Lackritz and Singh (2011) examined the moderating effect of big five personality on the relationship between role conflict, role ambiguity and burnout (emotional exhaustion, depersonalization and personal accomplishment). Data was collected from 263 faculty members of state university. Results of the study revealed that, extraversion is related with reduced emotional exhaustion and it plays a moderating role on the relationship of role conflict and personal accomplishments.

Dijkstra, Dierendonck, Evers, and Dreu De (2005) investigated the moderating role of extraversion on conflict and well-being of employees. Data was collected from 308 employees working in manufacturing sector of Netherland. Data was analyzed through descriptive analysis, correlations and hierarchical regression analysis. Results of the analysis indicated that, extraversion is negatively related to conflict and positively related to the well-being of the employees. Apart from this, extraversion has a moderating effect on the relationship of frequency of conflict and well-being of the employees. Employees having high extraversion trait experience less conflict and more well-being than employees having low in extraversion trait.

The results of present study and existing literature can be seen from the perspective of conservative of resource theory (COR). Since, extraversion has emerged as a strong moderator, which has a potential to contribute positively in work-life balance and mental health of employees, it can be considered as personal resource for employees, which they can utilize in crisis situations.

6.1.4.2. Agreeableness: The trait agreeableness describes someone who is cooperative, sympathetic, altruistic, compliant, kind, forgiving and trusting (McCrae & John, 1992). In the present research, moderating role of agreeableness was examined on the relationship of work-life balance and psychological distress and, work-life balance and psychological well-being of women managers. From Table 5.10 it has been found that the interaction between work-life balance and agreeableness (WLB x AGR) on psychological distress is significant (p=0.01), which confirmed the moderating role of agreeableness on the relationship of work-life balance and psychological distress of women managers. Similarly, from Table 5.11 it has been found that the interaction between work-life balance and agreeableness (WLB x AGR) on psychological well-being is also significant (p=0.01), which indicated that agreeableness has a moderating effect on the relationship of work-life balance and psychological well-being of women managers.

The findings are in the line of existing literature. According to Greenhaus and Beutell (1985), strain, contradictory work demands and absence of support results in work-family conflict. The characteristics associated with agreeableness lead to less interpersonal conflict and more support from co-workers and family members, which help in achieving good work-life balance. According to Zellars & Perrewe (2001), individuals high in agreeableness receive greater emotional support from family members and co-workers, due to which they experience less strain and more success in different domains of life.

Kinnunen, Vermulst, Gerris and Makikangas (2003) examined the moderating role of personality on the relationship between work-family conflict and well being of 296 full-time employed fathers in Netherland. Moderating effect of all five dimensions of personality was examined through hierarchical multiple regression analysis. Results of the analysis indicated that, agreeableness has moderating effect on the relationship between family interference with work (FIW) and marital satisfaction. Besides the moderating effect, agreeableness also had the main effect on well-being of employees.

Dijkstra, Dierendonck, Evers, and Dreu De (2005) investigated the moderating role of agreeableness on conflict and well-being of employees. Data was collected from 173 members of nursing and ancillary staff of a geriatric hospital. Analytical strategy included correlation analysis and hierarchical multiple regression analysis. Results of the study revealed that, agreeableness was negatively related with the conflict and the relationship was significant. In addition, agreeableness had a moderating effect on the relationship between conflict and individual well-being. Simple slopes of the regression lines revealed that conflict was negatively related to well-being only when individuals are low in agreeableness. The relationship is not the same for individuals high in agreeableness. This finding indicates that agreeableness protects the individual's well-being from the negative effect of conflict. Furthermore, authors concluded that people on high agreeableness interpret and perceive conflict situations in a positive way, which helps them in maintaining social relationships and prevent them from experiencing negative consequences of conflict on their well-being.

The results of present research and existing literature confirm the strong connection of agreeableness with work-life balance, social relationships with family members and co-workers and, individual's well-being. Hence, from the perspective of conservation of resource theory we can conclude that agreeableness is a personal resource, which positively contribute to work-life balance and mental health of women managers.

6.1.4.3. Conscientiousness: The trait conscientiousness describes someone who is achievement oriented, hard working, efficient, organized, dependable, responsible, and systematic (Judge & Higgins, 1999; McCrae & John, 1992). In the present research, moderating role of conscientiousness was examined on the relationship of work-life balance and psychological distress and, work-life balance and psychological well-being of women managers. From Table 5.12 it has been found that the interaction between work-life balance and conscientiousness (WLB x Cons) on psychological distress is significant (p=0.01), which confirmed the moderating role of conscientiousness on the relationship of work-life balance and psychological distress of women managers. Similarly, from Table 5.13 it has been found that the interaction between work-life balance and conscientiousness (WLB x Cons) on psychological well-being is also significant (p=0.02), which indicated that conscientiousness has a moderating effect on the relationship of work-life balance and psychological well-being of women managers.

The above findings can be discussed under the light of existing literature. Wayne et. al. (2004) investigated the relationship of Big Five personality traits and conflict and facilitation between work and family domains on the sample of 2130 participants from diverse occupational sector in USA. Results of the study indicated that, conscientiousness is negatively related with work-family conflict and family-work conflict while positively related with family-work facilitation. The authors argued that, characteristics of conscientiousness; careful planning, time management and effective organization, make a person capable of accomplishing more task in less time, which reduces incompatible time pressure, stress and strain which eventually leads to less conflict between work and family roles. Furthermore, successful accomplishment of task in one domain transfers positive mood and energy to another domain, which results in facilitation.

Judge, Higgins, Thoresen and Barrick (1999) investigated the relationship between Big five personality traits, general mental ability and career success across the life span. Data were obtained from three longitudinal intergenerational studies by the Institute of Human Development, University of California at Berkeley. Career success was measured on the dimensions of intrinsic success (job satisfaction) and extrinsic success (income and occupational status). Results of the study revealed that there is a significant positive correlation between conscientiousness, general mental ability and both the dimensions (intrinsic and extrinsic) of career success. Apart from this, conscientiousness had emerged as a significant predictor of job satisfaction. The authors have argued that, three characteristics of conscientiousness; achievement orientation (persistent & hardworking), dependability (careful & responsible) and orderliness (planful & organized) are related to individual's degree of self control and need for achievement, which make the construct (conscientiousness) a strong predictor of career success.

Barrick and Mount (19991) investigated the relationship of Big five personality dimensions (Extraversion, emotional stability, agreeableness, conscientiousness and openness to experience) with three criteria of job performance (job proficiency, training proficiency, and personnel data) for five major occupational groups; professionals, police, managers, sales and skilled/semi-skilled workers. Data were obtained from 117 studies, yielding 23, 994 participants for the study. Results of the study revealed that conscientiousness was a significant predictor of all three criteria of performance for all the occupational groups. Thus, this dimension of personality appeared to tap characteristics important to accomplish work tasks successfully in all occupational groups.

From the above discussed it can be concluded that, the trait conscientiousness can be considered as personal resource, which can be utilized in accomplishing tasks efficiently in work and family domains, which will have positive contribution in achieving work-life balance and maintaining good mental health.

6.1.4.4. Openness: The trait openness is characterized by intelligence, creativity, curiosity, unconventionality, imagination and originality (Barrick & Mount,1991; McCrae & John,1992). In the present research, moderating role of openness was examined on the relationship of work-life balance and psychological distress and, work-life balance and psychological well-being of women managers. From Table 5.14 it has been found that the interaction between work-life balance and openness (WLB x Open) on psychological distress is not significant (p=0.06), which indicated that, openness has no moderating effect on the relationship of work-life balance and psychological distress of women managers. Again, from Table 5.15 it has been found that the interaction between work-life balance and openness (WLB x Open) on psychological well-being is also not significant (p=0.08), which indicated that openness has not a moderating effect on the relationship of work-life balance and psychological well-being of women managers as well.

The other researchers have found similar kind of results in their studies. For example, Wayne et. al. (2004) investigated the relationship of Big Five personality traits and conflict and facilitation between work and family roles on the sample of 2130 participants from diverse occupational sector in USA. Results of the study indicated that, Openness was neither related to work-family conflict (WFC) nor to family- work conflict (FWC). However, it was positively related to work-family facilitation (WFF), but not to family-work facilitation (FWF). Hence, the trait openness was partially related to overall construct of work-life balance (WLB). Bruck and Allen (2003) investigated the relationship between Big five personality traits, negative affectivity, type A behavior, and different forms of work-family conflict (time, strain and behavior based conflict). The study was conducted on 164 employees working in different sector of organizations in USA. From the results it has been found that openness was not related to any form of work-family conflict, which indicated that the trait openness has no any impact on work-life balance of employees.

Furthermore, Ghorpade et.al (2011) examined the moderating role of personality on the relationship between role conflict, role ambiguity and burnout (emotional exhaustion, depersonalization & personal accomplishments). The study was conducted on 263 full-time faculty members of major universities in California. Data was analyzed through correlation, stepwise regression and moderation analysis. While analyzing the interaction of openness with role ambiguity on emotional exhaustion, it has been found that role ambiguity is positively related with emotional exhaustion and the effect is greatest for employees having high openness followed by employees having moderate degree of openness and least for employees having low degree of openness. It has been also found that above the mean level of role ambiguity the positive attenuating effect of openness disappeared. In fact, the degree of emotional exhaustion was highest when role ambiguity and openness to experience were both high. To explain the above phenomenon, authors argued that employees with high degree of openness and high perception of role ambiguity are more likely to get distracted from their work, which leads to greater emotional exhaustion (Lazarus & Folkman, 1984) and lower subjective well-being (DeNeve & Cooper, 1998).

The above discussion shows that, though openness is a positive personality trait, it is weakly related to work-life balance, which does not influence the relationship between work-life balance and mental health of women managers. In fact, high degree of openness makes employee more vulnerable to role ambiguity and emotional exhaustion. Hence, from the perspective of conservation of resource theory, it can be concluded that, openness does not act as personal resource in balancing work and personal life.

6.1.4.5. Neuroticism: The trait neuroticism refers to anxiety, worry, tension, insecurity and defensiveness (Judge & Higgins; McCrae & John, 1992). In the present research, moderating role of neuroticism was examined on the relationship of work-life balance and psychological distress and, work-life balance and psychological well-being of women managers. From Table 5.16 it has been found that the interaction between work-life balance and neuroticism (WLB x NEUR) on psychological distress is not significant (p=0.19), which indicated that, neuroticism has no moderating effect on the relationship of work-life balance and psychological distress of women managers. Again, from Table 5.17 it has been found that the interaction between work-life balance and neuroticism (WLB x NEUR) on psychological well-being is also not significant (p=0.08), which indicated that neuroticism has no moderating effect on the relationship of work-life balance and psychological well-being of women managers as well.

The obtained results are in the line of existing literature. Blanch and Aluja (2009) analyzed the interaction of work and family situational variables with big five personality traits in prediction of work-family conflict. The study was conducted on 694 married full time employees. From the analysis, neuroticism has emerged as strong predictor of work interference with family (WIF) and family interference with work (FIW). Similarly, Wayne et. al. (2004) investigated the relationship of Big Five personality traits and conflict and facilitation between work and family roles on the sample of 2130 employees in USA. Results of the study indicated that, neuroticism is positively related with both direction of conflict i.e. work-family conflict and family-work conflict. It has been also found that neuroticism is not related to work-family facilitation. To explain these relationship authors argue that the characteristics of neuroticism make individuals experience more work and family stress, which leads to higher conflict between the roles (Stoeva et.al. 2002). Furthermore, neurotics spend more time in worrying and focusing on negative side of situations, hence they have less time for accomplishing work and family tasks. Inefficient time management, greater preoccupation with role demands and higher perception of stress make them experience more conflict and less facilitation (Wayne et.al. 2004).

In context of mental health, it has been found that neuroticism is negatively related to life satisfaction and happiness while positively related to negative affect (DeNeve & Cooper, 1998). Neurotic individuals experience more emotional instability and show characteristics of worrying, sadness, guilt, fear, anger and embarrassment which eventually lead to negative affect and stress (Costa & McCrae, 1980).

From the above discussion and perspective of conservation of resource theory, it can be concluded that neuroticism cannot be considered as personal resource as it does not contribute in balancing work and personal life, rather it leads to more work-family conflict and stress in employees.

6.2. Section II : Qualitative Data Inference

The qualitative study was conducted on 8 participants, representing the different life stages of women managers. To know the work-life balance and mental health issues of women managers, five research questions were formulated. Data was obtained through face-to-face semi-structured interviews. After collecting the data, analysis was done through Interpretive Phenomenological Analysis (IPA) technique, from which 4 clusters, 10 themes and 24 sub-themes have emerged (Table 5.18).

The findings of qualitative study in the form of clusters, themes and subthemes are discussed below:

6.2.1. Cluster 1: Meaning of work-life balance

From the interviews of 8 women managers, it has been found that different individuals perceive their work-life balance differently. Everyone define work-life balance on their own way and attach specific meaning to it. For most of the participants meaning of work-life balance is derived from individual perception and individual experiences. Under this cluster two themes and six sub-themes have emerged:

Theme 1: Individual perception

According to Oxford dictionary, perception is the ability to understand or interpret any phenomenon (external stimuli) through our senses. It reflects the underlying belief and insight to view any situation. When participants were asked "How do you perceive your work-life balance?" varied kind of responses was recorded. Everyone defined their work-life balance differently. For some participants it was fulfilling needs of work and personal life, whereas some defined their work-life balance in context of happiness.

Sub-theme 1: Work and family needs- Most of the participants defined their work-life balance in context of fulfilling needs of work and personal life. For instance, one of the participants explained her work-life balance as *"If I fulfill my duties at home as well as at my workplace, I consider my work and personal life are balanced."* Another participant says, *I fulfill my duties at home as well as at my workplace, so I am satisfied with my work-life balance."* This subtheme highlights that, women managers place equal importance to work and home in their life. Though life includes other domains like finances, spiritual, hobbies, social and health as well, but work and family have emerged as most important domains in defining work-life balance for women managers.

Sub-theme 2: Happiness- For some participants feeling of happiness was crucial to define their work-life balance. If they are happy with their work and personal life they consider that, they have achieved a good work-life balance. For instance one of the participants says *"For me work-life is being happy with my work and my personal life".* According to Gropel and Kuhl (2009) work-life balance is positively related with subjective well-being (happiness) and this relationship is mediated by need fulfillment.

When work-life balance leads to fulfillment of needs at work and personal life, it positively contributes to person's happiness. Need fulfillment also creates a sense of goal achievement in the individuals which leads to happiness (Sheldon & Elliot, 1999). For instance one of the participants says "*In spite of my work, I am able to pursue my hobbies, it gives me happiness.*

Theme 2: Individual experience

Some of the participants defined their work-life balance according to their individual experience of work and personal life. For some participants work and personal life was never balanced, they experienced higher degree of work-family conflict, whereas some experienced more facilitation than conflict. Everyone had their own story to share; it was more like a personal journey. An interesting finding was that, the experience of work-life balance was greatly influenced by the life stages of the women managers. Women having small kids were more juggling with work and family life in comparison to unmarried and women with grown up kids.

Sub-theme 1: Conflict – When demands of work and personal life contradict with each other or become incompatible in some respects, conflict arises (Greenhaus & Beutell, 1985). It creates lots of stress and tension which hampers individual's work-life balance. While discussing the work-life balance of women managers, it has been found that many of the participants experience conflict between the work and family life. One of the participants says "*My work and personal life have never been balanced. There is so much work overload that I mentally carry my office work to home, which adversely affects my personal life.*" Participants also discussed about the time constraint, lack of quality time for family and responsibility for children and dependent elders. Explaining about the conflict, another participant says *"My parents have health issues; sometimes I have to leave them due to work."* This sub-theme represents an important dimension of work-life balance, which is well researched in work-family literature.

Sub-theme 2: Facilitation- Where some participants explained their work-life balance in context of conflict, other participants explained their work-life balance in context of facilitation as well. According to them, work and family positively contribute to each other. For instance, one of the participants says *"work provides financial support for the family, it improves quality of life"* Another participant says *"You can work only if your family is supportive. During March closing, I remain super busy in the office, reach late at home, but my family understands my job demands and takes care of the home responsibilities."* The facilitation (enhancement) is not only directed from work to family only, some participants consider that work has a positive contribution in their personal growth as well. For example, one of the participant shares *"Work gives me opportunity to learn"*. Hence, this theme represents a larger picture of facilitation, which includes work, family, self and other domains of life. However, in literature only work-family facilitation (WFF) and family-work facilitation (FWF) are explored (Greenhaus & Powell, 2006; Guest, 2002)

Sub-theme 3: Personal journey- Regarding work-life balance, every participant had their own story to share. It was more like a personal journey of work and family life. One of the participants says *"Work and family go hand-in-hand. If I would not have been working, my life would be a miserable life."* This sub-theme shows that people integrate their work and personal life as per their choice and lifestyle. Some people are "work centric" while for some "family comes first". There is no set formula, which is applicable to everyone. For instance, one of the participants says *"I have chosen to be a working woman, then why to crib for the challenges. I enjoy my work."* Another participant says *"family is the priority; we work to live not live to work"* Hence, meaning of work-life balance is all about enjoying one's own personal journey.

6.2.2. Cluster 2: Social support

Social support has emerged as another important cluster from the interviews of all the participants. All participants agreed that, without social support achieving work-life balance is almost an impossible task. It is well established fact that social support plays a significant role in balancing work and personal life (Buddhapriya, 2009; Rosenbaum and Cohen, 1999). During the interviews participants talked about the different form of social support which included role of family (spouse support, siblings support & in-laws support) and role of others (Domestic help & childcare support).

Theme 1: Role of family

Family plays the most significant role in balancing work and personal life for women managers. It provides instrumental, moral and emotional support to the managers in case of conflict between work and family life. Family members like spouse, siblings, parents and in-laws help in fulfilling the family demands, when the employee is on the duty at workplace.

Sub-theme 1: Spouse support- While talking about family support, most of the married participants appreciated the spouse support in balancing their work and family roles. Spouse plays a crucial role in taking care of child and providing moral and emotional support to the working women. For instance one of the participants says *"I live in nuclear family. My spouse is very supportive, that's why I am working"*. Apart from this, spouse also plays a significant role in establishing a cordial relationship between daughter-in-law and in-laws. For example, one of the participants says *"Spouse is very-very important in achieving your work-life balance, because he is the mediator between you and the in-laws and setting the expectations right."* Another participant says *"When there are lots of expectations coming on me, my husband settles the argument between me and my mother-in-law."* This sub-theme highlights the importance of spouse support in balancing work and family life for women managers, which is also emphasized in previous research (Aycan & Eskin, 2005; Roxburgh, 1999).

Sub-theme 2: In-laws support- For working daughter-in-law, in-laws are the assets. Most of the married women managers who lived in joint family mentioned the importance of in-laws support in their life to achieve work-life balance. For instance one of the participants says *"When I come to office, my mother-in-law takes care of my one and half year old son."* Another participant says *"I share a special bonding with my mother-in-law. She understands my work demands and helps me in taking care of child and other household works."* This theme changes the perception of living with in-laws as difficult task. Cordial relationships, mutual respect and right kind of expectations make life easier for working women living in joint family.

Theme 2: Role of others

Apart from family, there are other resources which provide instrumental support for women managers in achieving their work-life balance. In conversation with women managers, they talked about domestic help, child care facilities etc. to make their life easier. Being in higher income group, they are much capable in availing these facilities in comparison to women working in lower cadre.

Sub-theme 1: Domestic help- Almost all the participants talked about the domestic help to take care of the household chores. It provides the most significant instrumental support to women managers in fulfilling their home duties. Everyday household chores like cooking, cleaning, washing clothes etc. are taken care by domestic helps, which eases the burden of household works and enable the women more focused on work . For example, one of the participants says *"I don't take extra load from work as well as from home side. Cook comes and cooks the food for the family."* Another participant says *"I compromise with the taste of food made by my cook, because I know it is a great help."* This sub-theme highlights the importance of domestic help in the life of women managers, which is less mentioned in work-life balance literature. Studies rarely include role of domestic help, even though people often use it as instrumental support (Abendroth & Den Dulk, 2011).

Sub-theme 2: Childcare facilities- Women managers having small kids and living in nuclear family are not privileged with parental or in-laws support. They rely on outsourced childcare facilities like crèche, day care etc. For instance, one of the participants who live in nuclear family shares *"The school has crèche facility. After school my daughter stays in crèche, while I am in office."* This kind of facilities is indeed a great support to working women in balancing work and family life. It ensures the safety of child and provides peace of mind to the mother working at office. Lack of satisfactory childcare facility is one of the prime reasons for women managers to leave the job (Rosin & Korabik, 1990). Hence, satisfactory childcare support helps in reducing work-family conflict (Ahmad, 2002) and enhances job performance and satisfaction (Aryee & Luk, 1996).

6.2.3. Cluster 3: Organizational culture

When the participants were asked that "What is the role of your organization in achieving a good work-life balance?" all of the participants mentioned that it is the "organizational culture" which drives the formulation of work-life balance policies and its effective implementation in the organization. All organizations are not equally supportive, however work-life balance policies are almost everywhere. The degree of support one's get from organization is greatly influenced by the prevailing culture in the organization.

Under the umbrella of organizational culture employees get organizational support in the form of work-life balance policies and other family friendly programs which provide a great help to employees, but there are informal groups in the organization which play a signification role in helping employees to achieve their work-life balance.

Theme 1 : Organizational Support

In conversation with women managers they talked about formal and informal kind of support they get from their organizations to support their work-life balance. Both kind of support are equally emphasized in work-family literature, which have a great influence in the work-life balance of employees ((Abendroth & Den Dulk, 2011; Mahal, 2014).

Sub-theme 1: Formal support- Organizations provide formal support to their employees in the form of work-life balance policies and programs. These policies are explicitly written in the form of rules or ordinances, through which employees avail family friendly benefits. For example one of the participants says *"The organization provides family friendly policies like maternity leaves, childcare leaves and child education allowances etc."* Another participant says *"Organization is a big support. We get maternity leaves and childcare leaves in all PSUs. Childcare leaves are around 300 or 350 leaves per child till the 18 years of your child. You can take it in a go or in buckets."* This kind of formal support empowers women in dealing with difficult times and fulfilling the demands of work and family life (Aycan & Eskin, 2005; Thomas & Ganster, 1995)

Sub-theme 2- Informal support

Apart from formal support, employees get informal kind of support from their seniors and supervisors, which have a great value in achieving work-life balance. Again, the organizational culture defines the degree of informal support one's get from their supervisor. For example, one of the participants says *"If there is any emergency at home, we just call or message our senior. There is an understanding in the culture."* Another participant shares *"My son was sick and I took unplanned leave. At that time, I was supposed to be in a training program. I called up my senior and told that it is difficult for me to come, he said it's OK, you take care of your son and come back on work when he is fine, and he handled the training program on behalf of me."* The positive contribution of supervisor support in context of work-life balance is well mentioned in the literature. Supervisors help employees in interpreting work-family policies (Eby et al., 2002) and provide emotional support through empathetic understanding and listening work-family issues and showing genuine concern for the employee and his or her family (Frone et al., 1997)

Theme 2: Informal group

Informal groups are integral part of organizational culture. While talking to women managers, they mentioned the role of informal group in balancing their work and family life. These groups mainly comprise of colleagues who work together. The inter-personal relationship with colleagues and the communication flow across them greatly influence the work-life balance of employees.

Sub-theme 1: Role of colleagues

According to the participants, colleagues are big support in handling office works if it clashes with family demands. They provide instrumental support by assisting in work and giving advice to help the person getting out from the difficult situations. They also provide emotional support by giving empathetic ears to work-family problems. For example, one of the participants says *"More than formal policies, it is your understanding with colleagues, which makes your life easier."* However, in context of work-life balance, role of colleague is very less discussed in the literature, but some of the authors say that role of colleague is even more important, where organizations lack adequate work-life balance policies or if present they are poorly implemented (Mahal, 2014).

Sub-theme 2: Effective communication

Effective communication across the employee, seniors and colleagues has great importance in handling difficult situations. While talking about the strategies and planning, women managers revealed the importance of effective communication across the hierarchy. For example, one of the participants says *"If I plan any leave, I inform my seniors as well as my juniors before hand, so that they manage and work doesn't suffer in my absence."* Similarly, another participant says *"I make very clear and assertive communication with my senior and juniors regarding work assignments, distribution etc."* These scripts highlight the importance of communication in planning work and family assignments, which helps in achieving a better balance between work and family life.

6.2.4. Cluster 4 : Work-life balance and Mental health

When participants were asked "What is the impact of your work-life balance on your mental health?" they all agreed that there is an impact of work-life balance on their mental health. When there is a conflict between work and personal life, it has a negative impact on mental health, whereas when there is balance between work and personal life, it has a positive impact on mental health. Another question was asked as "What strategies you follow to achieve a good work-life balance and mental health?" Answering to this question, participants talked about their individual strategies to achieve better work-life balance and mental health, which included time management, exercise, recreational activities etc.

Theme 1: Impact of conflict on mental health

Participants explained that, work and personal life is not always balanced, sometimes they have to deal with the conflict between the two domains. When the degree of conflict is high, it affects their mental health in negative way. Most of the participants reported experiencing stress and burnout in juggling with work and personal life.

Sub-theme 1 : Stress- Almost all the participants talked about stress when dealing with conflict between work and personal life. In common, stress was the outcome of work-overload, pending works at home, longer working days etc. For example, one of the participants says *"When work load is high, I feel overburdened and stressed."* Another participant says *"When there is six days working in office, home works remain pending, it creates stress in my mind."* Research says, the importance of achieving a good work-life balance is directly related to the individual's overall level of stress. Those who are able to achieve balance between work and personal life experience lower level of stress than those who lack this balance (Karkoulian, Srour & Sinan, 2016; Ross & Vasantha, 2014).

Sub-theme 2 : Burnout- According to Leatz and Stolar (1993) " Burnout is a physical, emotional and mental exhaustion caused by long-term involvement in stressful and emotionally demanding situations, combined with high personal expectations for one's performance." While in conversation with women managers, some of the participants stated that, when the degree of conflict between work and family life is very high, they get exhausted and reached to the state of burnout. For example, one of the participants says *"Sometimes I feel so much overloaded that I tell my boss, that I will not be able to handle that much work".* Another participant says *"At office, if someone tries to pile me with work, I make a clear conversation that this much I can handle and this much I can't, similarly at home I make clear to my family members about my ability to handle the workload, otherwise I feel exhausted."* Juggling with family responsibilities and work overload requires lots of energy and ideal psychological state, failing to achieve this leads to physical and emotional exhaustion (Karatepe & Tekinkus, 2006).

Theme 2: Impact of balance on mental health

Besides conflict, participants also discussed about positive impact of work-life balance on their mental health. They consider work and family as integral part of their life, when there is proper balance between the two domains, they feel satisfied. Being able to work in spite of having family and child responsibilities, these women feel empowered and experience positive outcomes of work-life balance as discussed below:

Sub-theme 1: Sense of achievement- When there is proper balance between work and personal life, people enjoy their work. They feel proud of being working along with a family life. For example, one of the participants says *"My mental health is healthy because I am working. Being a kind of person I am, it is difficult for me to sit at home and doing nothing."* Another participant says *"I get pleasure, feeling proud of my work."* Hence, work provides a sense of achievement to these women managers, which positively impact their mental health.

Sub-theme 2: Self- identity- Some of the participants reported that, job makes them self-dependent. They feel good about being a working women, it gives them self- identity in social life. For example, one of the participant shares *"Kaam kar ke achha lagta hai, I have my own identity, I can take decisions myself.* Another participant says *"My parents always wanted me to become independent. It gives you your own identity in life, I feel proud about it."* This theme highlights the importance of work in empowering the women. It makes women self-sustained and independent in life.

Sub-theme 3: Contentment- Another outcome of work-life balance is reported as "contentment". According to some participants good balance between work and family life give them satisfaction, and make their life more content. For example one of the participants says *"I enjoy my work and I am very much satisfied with my life"*. According to Ryan and Deci (2001), a balanced life gives a psychological experience of control over work and family demands which helps in reducing stress and generating the feeling of contentment, which is an important parameter of employee's well-being and mental health.

Theme 3: Strategies for achieving good work-life balance

When participants were asked "What strategies you follow to achieve a good work-life balance"? They answered that they use multiple strategy in life to achieve a good work-life balance. Most of the participants talked about "Prioritizing" and "Time management" as two important strategies, which are very helpful in balancing their work and personal life.

Sub-theme 1: Prioritizing – According to some participants, prioritizing helps in planning day-to-day activities. The everyday "To-do list" is prepared on the basis of importance attached to particular work. Sometimes personal works are on the priority, while some other time office work may be the priority. One of the participants says *"I prioritize office and personal works as per their importance and urgency"*. Prioritizing is an important step of strategic planning, which helps in handling more tasks in less time. According to Ford and Collinson (2011), managers often prioritize their work to manage multiple tasks at office and home to achieve a good work-life balance.

Sub-theme 2: Time management – It is another important strategy, women managers adopt in balancing their work and family life. Multiple responsibilities at work and home require effective utilization of time. For instance, one of the participants says *"After finishing my work at office, I rush for home. I never waste my time in office gossips."* Time management is the skill of creating time budgets, allocating time to assigned tasks and efficient use of 24 hours of the day. It enables managers to become multitasking and give quality time to their work and family life.

Theme 4 : Strategies for good mental health

When participants were asked "What strategies you follow to maintain good mental health"? They talked about multiple strategies like; exercise, meditation, recreation and open communication. These strategies help them in releasing fatigue, burnout and negative emotions which have a positive impact on their mental health.

Sub-theme 1: Exercise – Regular exercise helps in reducing stress and keeping the mind and body healthy. Participants reported exercise as one of the strategies to stay fit and healthy. For example one of the participants says *"I do regular exercise to stay physically and mentally fit."* Another participant says, *"I go to gym early in the morning, it gives me energy for rest of the day"*. Fulfilling multiple responsibilities at work and home requires lots of energy and stamina, only a healthy mind and body can handle these life demands. Hence, doing regular exercise is a good practice to feel energetic and stay healthy.

Sub-theme 2: Meditation- Meditation is another important practice which women managers do to stay calm and healthy. It helps in reducing stress, anxiety and pain. For example, one of the participants says *"I used to be very stressed in handling multiple responsibilities. To get the peace of mind, I have started meditation."* As mentioned in literature conflict between work and personal life leads to perceived stress, mood and anxiety disorders and females are more vulnerable with these kinds of disorders (Wang Li, 2006). Meditation generates awareness and mindfulness in the individual which helps in reducing stress and restoring healthy balance between work and family life.

Sub-theme 3: Recreational activities- Taking a short break from the work and engaging in recreational activities also helps in reducing stress and gaining new energy. As reported by the participants, recreational activities are necessary to overcome the burnout generated from work and family life. For example, one of the participants says *"I need outings in every two or three months, otherwise I feel irritated and exhausted"*. Another participant says *"If I feel stressed, I go for brisk walk and listen music"*. According to Greenblatt (2002), recreational activities like small trips, picnic or short vacation with family, help employees to rejuvenate and stay mentally healthy.

Sub-theme 4: Open communication- It is another useful strategy, which helps in distressing women managers from battle of work-life balance. As reported by participants, open communication with supervisors, co-workers and family members help them sharing their worries and resolving problems. For example one of the participant shares *"If I feel stressed I vent out my feelings to my family members"*. Open communication also helps in releasing negative emotions like fear, anger, frustration etc. which leads to better mental health outcomes.

7.1. Summary

The present study shows work-life balance from psychological perspective by focusing on mental health of women managers. Today mental illness in workforce is a global challenge. The World Federation for Mental Health (WFMH) on the occasion of World Mental Health day, 2017 addressed the key theme "Mental Health in the Workplace", in which it was reported that at global level, one-in-four people will likely to experience some kind of mental health problems at any stage of their lives. Around the world, over 300 million people are estimated to suffer from depression, which is equivalent to 4.4% of world's population and 800,000 people take their lives every year due to mental health problems (WFMH, 2017). This study has been chosen to conduct because, conflict between work and personal life is one of the prime reasons of developing mental illnesses in employees (Haar et. al., 2014; Wang Li, 2006). Organization must acknowledged that, the burden of managing work and family responsibility that women professionals face results in many negative mental and physical health outcomes. In today's organizations, where number of women professionals are constantly increasing, poor mental health adversely affect the pace of organizational growth. Hence, for optimum utilization of the talent of women professionals, organizations must show sensitivity towards their work-life balance and mental health issues. Though, all women professionals working in different hierarchy face problems of work-life balance, but women at managerial positions work under high pressure and job demands. At workplace they have the responsibility of leadership roles, while at home they still continue to have the primary responsibility of taking care of the children, dependent elders and household needs. Conflict between the multiple roles often leads to negative health outcomes including mental illnesses like stress, depression and anxiety disorders (Yucel, 2017; Wang Li, 2006). Hence, there is a need to explore potential moderators which can buffer the negative impact of conflict on the mental health of women managers. From the perspective of "Conservation of resource" theory emotional intelligence and personality characteristics can be assumed as personal resources which can weaken the negative impact of the conflict on the mental health of the individual. Thus, the present study examined the moderating role of emotional intelligence and personality on the relationship of work-life balance and mental health of women managers. It broadly studied the work-life balance and mental health issues of women managers working in different sector of organizations in Delhi/NCR through quantitative as well as qualitative method. The details of the study are presented in previous seven chapters, which are summarized as below:

The first chapter is about the introduction of the topic with special reference to current issues of work-life balance in today's organizations, importance of work-life balance in employees' life, recent changes in work-force demographics in India and women professionals working at managerial positions and their challenges. Since the women managers are constantly juggling with their work and personal life, which has a great impact on their mental health, these issues built up the foundation for the rationale of the study.

The second chapter introduced the all four variables under the study i.e. work-life balance, mental health, emotional intelligence and personality and explained their origin, evolution, important models and theories and their inter-relationship with each other with the help of existing literature. On the basis of their relationship and existing literature the theoretical framework (model) has been designed and relevant objectives and hypotheses were formulated.

The third chapter explained the method of conducting the study which included research design, participants and procedure, and details of tools used in data collection. Mixed method design (Convergent design, Wittink et al. 2006) has been used, in which 311 participants for quantitative analysis and 8 participants for qualitative analysis have been included. Four tools; work-life balance scale (Hayman, 2005), Mental health inventory (Weit & Ware, 1983), Emotional Intelligence Scale (Wong & Law, 2002) and Big Five Inventory (John and Srivastava, 1999) have been used to collect the data for quantitative inquiry, while semi-structured interviews were conducted to collect the data for qualitative inquiry.

The fourth chapter explained the validation of tools. Under this chapter, the structure of each tool has been validated through confirmatory factor analysis by using AMOS software. After validation, model fit indices, factors, items and their factor loadings of final version of each tool have been reported in the form of tables.

The fifth chapter explained the analyses part of the study which included both quantitative and qualitative analysis. Under quantitative analysis results of descriptive analysis (frequency& percentage of demographic variables, test for normality and t-test), correlation analysis and moderation analysis were reported, while under qualitative analysis, results of Interpretive Phenomenological Analysis (IPA) in the form of clusters, themes and sub-themes with supportive extracts were reported.

The sixth chapter extensively discussed the results of both quantitative and qualitative analysis. The chapter has been divided into two sections. Under section-I results of quantitative analysis were discussed in context of each formulated hypothesis and explained in the light of existing literature. Under section-II, results of qualitative analysis in the form of cluster, themes and sub-themes are discussed in hierarchical manner.

The important findings of quantitative analysis are as follows:

- To see the group difference between women managers working in government organizations and women managers working in private sector organization, t-test analysis was conducted, which revealed that there was significant difference on the dimensions of psychological distress, self emotion appraisal, agreeableness and consciousness between the groups. However, the two groups did not show any significant difference on the dimensions of work-life balance (work interference with personal life, personal life interference with work & work/personal life enhancement). In context of mental health, women managers working in private sector organizations scored high on psychological distress in comparison to women managers of government sector organizations. This difference exists due to the different kind of work culture prevailing in the two sectors. The government sector organizations provide more supportive environment to their employees . These findings provide useful insight to private sector organizations for improving their work culture and providing emotional intelligence training and personality development programs to their women managers, so that they become more capable of acquiring and utilizing their personal resources and stay mentally healthy.

- The Pearson product moment correlation analysis of the data revealed the relationship between the dimensions of study variables. It was found that there is a significant positive correlation between work-life balance and psychological well-being, while there is a significant negative correlation between work-life balance and psychological distress of women managers. Hence, work-life balance has emerged as an important factor which greatly impacts the mental health of women managers.

  It has been also found that emotional intelligence is significantly and positively related with work-life balance and psychological well-being, while negatively related with psychological distress. In context of personality factors, extraversion, conscientiousness, agreeableness and openness have been found to be positively related with psychological well-being and emotional intelligence and negatively related with psychological distress, while neuroticism has been found to be significantly and negatively related with work-life balance, psychological well-being and emotional intelligence, while positively related with psychological distress. Hence, it can be concluded that emotional intelligence, extraversion, conscientiousness, agreeableness and openness positively contribute to work-life balance and mental health of women managers, while neuroticism negatively impact their work-life balance and mental health.

- Findings of moderation analysis revealed four potential moderators which positively influence the work-life balance and mental health of women managers.

Emotional intelligence has emerged as first important moderator, which helps in achieving work-life balance in difficult situations. It has been found that managers having high emotional intelligence experience lesser psychological distress due to work-family conflict than managers having low emotional intelligence do. Hence, managers can utilize their emotional intelligence as personal resource to balance day to- day work and family demands without experiencing much psychological distress. By displaying a good emotional intelligence they can regulate their emotional and behavioral reactions at work and family life, which will not only make them less vulnerable to resource loss, but also enable them to better manage their stress caused by work and family issues.

- **Extraversion** has emerged as second potential moderator which positively influences the relationship between work-life balance and mental health of women managers. The characteristics of extraversion provide positivity and high energy to the individuals, which make them more competent in handling stressful situations. Being an extravert person, the individual focuses on the positive aspect of the situation and experience more facilitation than conflict. Hence, the trait extraversion can be utilized as personal resource to achieve good work-life balance and mental health.

- **Agreeableness** has emerged as third potential moderator which positively influences the relationship between work-life balance and mental health of women managers. The trait agreeableness makes a person more cooperative, sympathetic, kind and trusting. These characteristics help in building cordial interpersonal relationships with family members and co-workers which help in achieving good work-life balance.

- **Conscientiousness** has emerged as fourth potential moderator. The trait conscientiousness makes a person hard working, efficient, responsible and systematic. These characteristics help in careful planning, time management and effective organization, which are very useful in balancing work and personal life, without experiencing much pressure and strain.

Hence, women managers should focus on cultivating extraversion, agreeableness and conscientiousness in their personality to achieve better work-life balance and mental health.

The important findings of qualitative analysis are as follows:

- Qualitative study was done through Interpretive Phenomenological Analysis (IPA), which provided many important results in the form of clusters, themes and sub-themes. The four clusters emerged through the analysis are: Meaning of Work-life balance, Social support, Organizational culture, Work-life balance and Mental health.

The first cluster **"Meaning of work-life balance"** of qualitative analysis revealed that for each women manager work-life balance is a personal journey. Everyone perceives it differently and attaches different meaning to it. Some women managers experience more conflict while others may experience more facilitation in balancing work and personal life, which has a negative or positive influence on their mental health. Hence, individual characteristics play a crucial role in moderating work-life balance and mental health of these participants which is also supported by the results of quantitative analysis.

- The second cluster **"Social support"** talked about the role of family and role of others in contributing work-life balance of women managers. In context of role of family, spouse support has emerged as extremely important factor in supporting the career of women managers along with their family life. Besides, role of in-laws also play crucial role in taking care of children and other household needs, which   help women managers to achieve good balance between their work and family life.

  Apart from family members, outsourced resources like domestic help and crèche facilities also contribute significantly in easing the burden of household chores and childcare duties of women managers. These factors have emerged as great help in facilitating the work-life balance of women managers.

- The third cluster **"Organizational culture"** revealed the role of organizations in contributing the work-life balance of women managers. Under the umbrella of organizational culture, formal and informal kind of organizational support, role of colleagues and effective communication across the hierarchy have emerged as important factors which positively contribute to the work-life balance of women managers.

- The fourth cluster **"Work-life balance and mental health"** highlighted the different aspects of work-life balance and mental health. Women experienced stress and burnout due to conflict between work and personal life, but they also acknowledged sense of achievement, self-identity and contentment due to their work life. Hence, there is a mix kind of experience they feel, when they deal with their work-life balance issues.

At personal level, women managers also adopt useful strategies to cope up with day-to-day juggling of work and family demands. Prioritizing the tasks and time management are two important strategies, which they consider very useful in accomplishing multiple tasks of work and family life. These strategies make them more efficient in handling time pressure and high job demands. For good mental health they do regular exercise and meditation, go for recreational activities and believe in open communication with co-workers and family members. These practices help them in releasing negative emotions and rejuvenating their mental health.

7.2. Conclusion

Hence, from the study, it can be concluded that work-life balance is a personal journey for every women manager, which has a great impact on her mental health. To meet the demands of work and personal life, everyone strives to achieve a good balance between the two important domains of life. The results of the study say that, achieving a good work-life balance is yet a difficult, but not an impossible task. Effective utilization of personal resources like emotional intelligence, extraversion, agreeableness and consciousness can enable a person to achieve a good work-life balance without experiencing much psychological distress. Besides, availing right kind of social and organizational support and adopting useful strategies in life one can successfully achieve a good balance between work and personal life and stay mentally healthy.

7.3. Implications

The present study has both theoretical and practical implications, which are as follows:

1. Previous studies on work-life balance research were mainly confined to work-family conflict and family-work conflict. The present study goes beyond to explore work-personal life enhancement dimension of work-life balance and its impact on mental health of women managers, which meaningfully contribute to work-family body of literature.

2. The present study examines the potential moderators like emotional intelligence and personality on the relationship of work-life balance and mental health of women managers, which are less explored in the literature of work-life balance.

3. The present study examines the moderating role of emotional intelligence and personality from the perspective of "Conservation of Resource" (COR) theory, which tests the COR theory in Indian work-family culture and supports its generalizability beyond the western culture.

4. The study highlights the importance of emotional intelligence, which is very crucial in handling personal and work-place issues. It helps in establishing good inter-personal relationships at work-place as well as with family members, which positively contribute to one's work-life balance. Hence organizations can provide emotional intelligence training and interventions to their employees to make them more emotionally intelligent in handling work and family issues.

5. The study also explains the importance of extraversion, agreeableness and consciousness in achieving good work-life balance. Organization can conduct interventions and personality development programs to improve these resources

of employees to make them more competent in balancing their work and personal life.

6. The study also talks about important strategies of achieving good work-life balance and maintaining mental health. The employees, especially women can be educated and trained on these strategies to become more capable of improving their work-life balance and mental health.

7.4. Limitations

Like any other study, the present study also has some limitations, which are as follows:

1. The data for the present study is collected from Delhi and NCR only, future studies can be conducted across the country with larger sample size.

2. Tools used in the study for data collection were self-reporting questionnaires; Future scholars can conduct the study by using peer-reporting measures which **can tap respondent's parameters** through different sources like family members, super-visors and co-workers.

3. The group difference is studied on the basis of type of organization only, other demographic variables like marital status, type of family, number of children and dependent elders etc. can also be taken into account to study the difference between the groups.

4. The qualitative part of study was conducted through open-ended questions; the participants had more control over the content of the data collected. Hence the results may be influenced through their subjective interpretations of the content, which cannot be verified or tested objectively.

7.5. Suggestions for future research

1. The present study has been conducted on women managers working in Delhi and NCR only, future research can be conducted across the country with larger sample size, so that a broader picture of work-life balance and mental health issues of women managers can be visualized.

2. Future studies can explore other moderators like mindfulness, job autonomy, and social support etc. on the relationship of work-life balance and mental health.

3. The present study explores the "spillover" phenomenon of work-life balance. Future studies can be conducted to explore "crossover" phenomenon of work-life balance.

4. The present study is conducted on the work-life balance of women managers only, future studies can take account of male managers as well, so that some gender related conclusions can be drawn.

5. Future studies can also be conducted on single parents, divorced and widow women to address their work-life balance and mental health issues.